a
girl's
life

MARIANNE GINGHER

a girl's life

horses
boys
weddings
& luck

Louisiana State University Press *Baton Rouge*

Copyright © 2001 by Louisiana State University Press
All rights reserved
Manufactured in the United States of America
First printing
10 09 08 07 06 05 04 03 02 01
5 4 3 2 1

Designer: Barbara Neely Bourgoyne
Typeface: Granjon and Amphion
Printer and binder: Thomson-Shore, Inc.

Library of Congress Cataloging-in-Publication Data:
Gingher, Marianne.
  A girl's life : horses, boys, weddings, and luck / Marianne Gingher.
    p. cm.
  ISBN 0-8071-2685-3 (cloth : alk. paper)
    1. Gingher, Marianne. 2. Young women—United States—Biography. 3. Middle class—
United States. I. Title.
  HQ1229.G55 G56 2001
  305.242'092—dc21

00-012117

Portions or variations of some of the essays included in this collection previously appeared
in *Family Fun, Veranda, Carolina Quarterly, NC Homes,* the *Oxford American,* the *Washington
Post Magazine,* and the anthologies *Close to Home* (Blair, 1996), *Summer* (Addison-Wesley,
1990), and *The Store of Joys* (Blair, 1997).

For Lawrence
Who nurtured this book into being

She measured her life according to what poured from the horn of plenty, which was her own seamless, ample, cascading, elastic, susceptible, inexact heart.

—Cynthia Ozick

A sheltered life can be a daring life as well. For all serious daring starts from within.

—Eudora Welty

Contents

METAPHORS AND PIES

Photographs

Acknowledgments

Thanks to my children, Rod and Sam Gingher, who are forever expanding the repertoire of my emotions and insights; and to my cousin, Lynn Preston, who is the true family historian and was the audience I often imagined when I wrote some of these pieces; and to my mother and brothers, who have verified much of this material and would agree that though I might exaggerate, I've not outright lied; and to Les Phillabaum and John Easterly at LSU Press for understanding that all happy families aren't necessarily alike; and to my friends and colleagues Daphne Athas, Doris Betts, and Linda Wagner-Martin for all their biases in my favor; and to Ellen Douglas for her significant enthusiasm; and to the Institute of Arts and Humanities at the University of North Carolina at Chapel Hill and the Max C. Chapman family for enrichment and support; and, finally, to the reviewer Michael Vincent Miller, who wrote the following in the *New York Times Book Review:* "Would someone please confess to having had simply a happy childhood that led forward to an adult life of fulfillment and well-being, even without Prozac? Now there would be a revelation!" I heeded his request, and here's the book.

a
girl's
life

SANCTUARY

A Hard Place to Get To

MOST EVERY SUMMER we went: my parents and assorted children, piling into the suitcase-jammed station wagon (pre-air-conditioned comfort, pre-disposable diaper, pre-Interstate highway) to make the arduous journey. From our home in piedmont North Carolina, Mount Vernon, Illinois—the town where my mother's parents lived—seemed a hard place to get to.

We left before dawn, the youngest often carried to the car in pajamas. My father, gabby with holiday spirit, wore a sports cap with upturned bill and clip-on sunglasses that he'd flip up from his monster horn-rims when he read road maps. Mother copiloted cheerfully beside him. Her job was to spot elusive route signs, to refold the maps that he shook loose, to scout out the cleanest-looking filling stations, and to peel my father sticks of chewing gum. He chain-chewed Juicy Fruit, its perky jelly-bean fragrance lightening the predawn air. As my mother ceremoniously offered him the first stick of the trip, his face turned rowdy and boyish. He inserted a key, mashed the gas pedal, hearkened to the drum roll of the Plymouth's engine—and we were off.

The first day we drove fourteen or fifteen hours on a two-lane road that roller-coasted through the Blue Ridge Mountains, the Great Smokies, and shot the Cumberland Gap into Tennessee. In Bristol we stopped for gasoline, Tru-Ades, butterscotch Life-Savers, more Juicy Fruit, and to use the rest rooms, if we hadn't already relieved ourselves in the mayonnaise jars my mother brought along. On one memorable descent into Bristol, our brakes failed and my father slunk the Plymouth in low gear all the way down the mountain, jerking the emergency brake like a joystick, heroically dragging one foot along the pavement, waving away with martyrlike grandeur the fresh stick of gum my mother unfurled.

Once the hazards of mountain driving were past, we sang the exuberant, swaggering songs of survivors: military airs, mostly. To commemorate our safe arrival into the flatlands of Tennessee, my mother sang "The Tennessee Waltz." Then my brothers begged my parents to sing "Bill Grogan's Goat"—even the gruesome verse in which the train engineer slits the poor goat's throat—and they merrily complied.

We chattered noisily about Daniel Boone and the pioneers who'd traveled this route by horseback, blazing the Wilderness Trail. We marveled at their courage and counted ourselves lucky to enjoy the relative speed and poshness of a modern concrete highway. Daddy pointed out historical markers, Civil War graveyards and battle sites. And if our attention drifted toward games of Counting Cows and License Plate Poker, he roused us with his cornball rendition of "Daddy's Whiskers":

> One morning at the breakfast table,
> Mommy had nothing to eat.
> She grabbed old Daddy's whiskers
> 'Cause she thought they were Shredded Wheat!
> They're always in the way,
> The cows eat them for hay,
> They hide the dirt on Daddy's shirt,
> They're always in the way!

We enjoyed high spirits until lunchtime—because it hadn't gotten hot yet.

It was the day's rising heat that dictated where and when we finally stopped to eat. We ritually chose a Howard Johnson's for their pistachio ice cream (triangular-shaped scoops served in frosty metal compotiers) and because all Howard Johnson's were air-conditioned. In the turquoise chill of the restaurant, we were as happy as fish in an aquarium, languishing over our luncheon plates long after our meal was finished and the youngest of my brothers had grown fidgety. Beyond the cool pane of Howard Johnson's window glass, the parking lot shimmered like a pancake griddle. To stall for time, we children even ate the crusts from our sandwiches.

We climbed back into the Plymouth whimpering, fussing, picking fights. We could feel the heat of the asphalt soaking through the rubber soles of our P. F. Flyers, melting them down. The sun, heavy as an iron, flattened the tops of our heads, and the interior of the unshaded Plymouth roared like a furnace. Our skin stuck to the upholstery; the baby was allowed to ride naked, without his diaper, if he promised to venture the mayonnaise jar.

We were finished with games, with pointing out Burma-Shave signs, with singing, with the esprit of pioneers. We scrunched away from each other so that we wouldn't stick together, folded our arms, and sulked. If we were lucky, we slept. The only things that roused us from our brooding stupor were the farm-sluggish smells of the countryside: hog and chicken lots, mud-brothy creeks, dead animals ripening along the bug-twangy, overlush roadside, smells you could taste in the back of your throat, that made you grind your teeth and wake up hollering for mercy.

We were covered in prickly heat rash. Once, when we stopped to buy ice cream near a town called French Lick, my brothers took their vanilla ice cream cones and painted big bull's-eyes on their bare stomachs for relief.

We were bound and determined to make London, Kentucky, before nightfall. And if my father now drove with a vengeance, if he broke the speed limit, it was because he knew, blessedly assured by his motor club guidebook, that waiting for us there was a spanking-new motel outfitted with air conditioners. It was called the London Hall.

London Hall, London Hall, we chanted as the miles ticked off. Surely we were much too sweaty and rumpled to enter such a place. My mother brought out a comb and slicked us all up, for we envisioned a castle with turrets, cool as stone. *London Hall, London Hall:* we breathed the hallowed incantation in each other's ears, on each other's rash-peppered necks, on the moist, closed eyelids of those of us still lucky enough to be sleeping.

At the London Hall Motor Inn, my father checked us all into a room as square and plain and white as the interior of an ice-cream carton. It was furnished with two double beds, a foldaway cot, and a couple of end tables equipped with Reader's Digests and Bakelite ashtrays. But what we saw, when we opened the door, paled in comparison with what we felt: air that clattered, it was so cold, air that dropped upon your shoulders like a metal cape, that went straight for your melted bones and ordered them instantly into solid, sentinel form.

A few seconds of exposure and we'd all raised goose bumps the size of thumbtacks. We plunged into the room, bouncing from one bed to the other. My parents bounced, too. My brothers snooped around, opening drawers, parting the shower curtain, tumbling on the carpet, which was as bright red and icy cold as cocktail sauce. The air conditioner blathered away full blast in one corner, as chatty-sounding as a good host. Frost glistened invitingly on its vents, and we kids scraped it off with our fingernails and ate it, smacking our lips, fluttering our eyelids with pleasure. None of us admitted when the cold became unbearable, but of course it did, and soon enough we were donning bathing suits and heading for the steamiest swimming pool in history.

To lie floating on my back in the London Hall Motor Inn swimming pool, thawing myself out from the arctic motel room, felt nothing short of prodigal: cows bellowing in the pasture (the pool was located next to a stockyard), an inkling of moon slipping into view, my family splashing close by, and supper wholeheartedly abandoned in favor of snacks levered from machines. This must have been my earliest brush with decadence. It never occurred to me, as I drifted on my back and stared up into the muggy twilight, watching the slow tufting of small, soft-looking summer stars, that we were little more than halfway to Mount Vernon.

Some summers my father couldn't take time away from his office to drive us, and so my mother dauntlessly shepherded us kids aboard the Southern Railway for a circuitous journey that involved a tricky connection in Atlanta. We were to change not only trains in Atlanta but train stations, too, a Houdini-esque maneuver my mother, with her brood of babies, managed only through the kindness of many strangers. Once we left the Southern and boarded the B & O line, we ratcheted along in our compartment for about eighteen hours—first aiming north toward Cincinnati, then west to Fort Wayne.

I remember these excursions as the greatest adventures of my childhood. Oh, those risky clamorous leaps between the bucking cars as we made our way to dinner. The naughty thrill of finding out that when you flushed the little toilets, their contents emptied on the track! And no sideshow extravagance could equal the daring with which the waiters in the dining car poured our milk. With one hand they'd decorously present an empty glass at child's-eye level. The other hand produced a carton of milk as if by a snap of fingers and, brandishing the carton high above the clattering table, took what looked to be improbable aim and poured. The milk purled down, a Niagara Falls of milk. We knew it was wet, that in seconds we'd be drinking it, and yet it seemed transformed into something solid as it swung between the waiter's hands, suspended like a rope of taffy or the whipped-out arc of a jump rope. The train swayed, but the milk looped steadily down the air. We barely had time to gasp before it filled its intended target. Not one drop spilled. Daredevil Milk, we called it, and gulped it greedily, the way Popeye gulped spinach. Of course we begged for second glasses, but my mother said one glass was enough. She claimed that the milk had an acrobatic influence, that they probably flavored it with Mexican jumping beans, and that one glass before bedtime made us tumbly enough.

After dinner, though it was barely dark, we retired to our roomette to wash hands and faces in the little birdbath sink and slip into beds the porters had made up. I snuggled into my upper berth, much too excited to sleep right away, content to lie there feeling cozy, listening to the click and chatter of train wheels, the whoosh of dark, silent farmland outside the shaded window, the plaintive ding-dang of crossings that quickly faded, absorbed into the nighttime otherness of towns we passed. Who knew where we were? Only the beast-of-burden train knew as it tunneled through the night. My sheets crackled with starch. I've never felt so well tended, dreamy with prospect, and as fearless about the unfamiliar since.

We arrived at sunrise—the train made a special stop for us at the crossroads of a dew-covered nowhere where my grandfather's big blue Imperial was parked beside a cornfield. Nearby stood my grandfather, wearing a jaunty straw hat, and my grandmother, rouged, in a swirly Sunday dress, a purse swinging on her arm.

As soon as we'd alighted from the train, my mother's stouthearted firmness relaxed, gave way to a kind of girlishness as she allowed herself to be a daughter again. We children were permitted to scamper, expected to devise our own amusements. So if we chose to spend a whole afternoon gouging tar out of a road and chewing it, nobody protested. You could goof off to your heart's content and nobody said a word, nobody ever asked you to account for your day. You could derive enormous pleasure simply from sitting on the front-porch glider all afternoon, watching cars cruise up and down North 12th Street, counting the convertibles. North 12th was paved with maroon-colored bricks, and the traffic made a rich lopping sound like beaters whirring cake batter.

Which might remind you to go pester Maggie, Granny's cook, about making a favorite dessert for supper and letting you help. All desserts were made from scratch, and they were culinary spectacles: twelve-egg angel food cake with cups of boiled custard on the side for dunking, Coronation Butterscotch Pie, Granny's Graham Cracker Roll, Hundred Dollar Chocolate Cake, which is how much a woman had offered to pay the chef for the recipe. At breakfast and dinner we

ate off Fiesta Ware, and my brothers and I always argued over who
got the cobalt-blue plate.

Roam, goof off, dawdle, snoop. I liked pilfering my Uncle Dick's
bedroom. He'd left home by the time we started making our pilgrim-
ages, but his bedroom remained intact with oddball treasures. He'd
ditched a first-rate collection of science fiction books and westerns and
a stack of RCA Victor records, big 78-rpm platters with burgundy-
and-silver labels. My favorite record was a song about a balky race-
horse named Beetlebaum. I was terrified of the name: the monstrous
bass thrum of the word "Beetlebaum" leaping off the record made my
heart pound. It sounded like a reprimand. But whenever I got the
chance to slip off to Uncle Dick's bedroom alone and put the record
on, I did. It was a test of some sort.

My brothers liked exploring the back alley, where Dada burned
trash in a huge ashcan. A bitter, licoricelike smell of smoke hovered
in the air, whether there was a fire or not. Sometimes we pretended
the ashes were snow and staged snowball fights with big, flaky handfuls. Beyond the alley was the Bunchmans' house and broad lawn
(they had six redheaded children) and a crooked little ankle-deep
creek loaded with crawdads and salamanders. Dada had strung a rope
swing from the maple tree that arched over the porte cochere. He'd
laid out a croquet court in the backyard amidst metal scalloped-back
lawn chairs and a fringed canvas hammock my brothers were always
flipping each other out of. There was a gravel driveway that you could
comb for hours, hunting mica specimens. In the basement stood deep
zinc wash sinks with black rubber hoses attached to the spigots, where
we children were encouraged to bathe. We liked to stuff the hose in
our mouths and pretend we were deep-sea divers hunting pearls.

Sometimes Dada would take us out in the little motorboat that he'd
built and painted himself. He'd let us mess with the tools in his garage
workshop; once he helped us build a triangular birdhouse that we
painted to resemble the Eiffel Tower. He taught us Parcheesi and told
us stories of his oil-rigging days in Oklahoma and about the time he
lost the tip end of one of his fingers in a piece of machinery. He talked
about his and Granny's elopement on his 1918 Harley-Davidson

motorcycle when she was still engaged to another boy back in Danville, Kentucky. He pulled half dollars out of our ears and *paid* my brothers for giving him back rubs. He called my oldest brother "Knothead" and they became best pals—the bestowing of a nickname will do that. Best of all, he let us watch him dress his stump, and once he let young Knothead do the honors.

Dada's stump was where one of his feet should have been. He'd lost the foot to a gangrenous infection. There wasn't anything scary about the stump except that it signaled an absent foot; we considered it a fleshly *contraption*.

The stump was round and smooth and pink like a small bald head, and Dada rubbed it with baby oil to keep it from drying out. He talked softly when he rubbed it, as if the stump were asleep. He said it was numb; he said you could stick a pin in it and he wouldn't feel pain, although he'd still bleed. After he oiled it, he dressed it in a special sock and a cup-shaped brace and attached it to one shoe.

He limped, of course, but it wasn't his stump that slowed him down. It was his lungs. He'd survived a terrible car crash when he was a young man. His chest had been crushed by the steering wheel, all his ribs broken, his lungs punctured, his jaw so mangled that they'd had to wire it back together, and he hadn't been expected to live. He loved to talk about surviving that wreck, how the doctors had hovered over him with grave predictions. But he'd outfoxed them, he'd say to us, slapping his knee, his struggle amply rewarded, for here we all were, years later, worshiping him.

We stayed in Mount Vernon for three or four weeks—sometimes longer. My mother got a tan. She and her old high school friends spent time together, playing golf, going to luncheons given in her honor. Much of the time we kids simply hung around the house with Granny and Dada, never feeling the need of things to do, never bored. It was the treasure-trove otherness of my grandparents' house that we relished and basked in. A kind of wealth awaited us there. It was a time of indiscriminate savoring, of not only detecting differences but plundering them for all their worth.

Dada read his newspaper, and for hours I could content myself watching him read. Unlike my father, Dada wetted a thumb to help him turn the pages. Now and then he would pause and adjust his reading glasses—there was a pleasant rhythm to this motion. He crossed his legs at the ankles, displaying the harlequin jigsaw designs of his Argyles. Whenever he read something in the paper that he didn't like, he'd shout, "Land!"

After I'd watched Dada awhile, I'd mosey into Granny's bedroom to find her seated at her vanity, arranging her hair. "You need a girl your own age to play with or you'll be *bored,*" she'd say. When she said the word "bored" she bugged her eyes as if she'd swallowed poison. But I liked "bored." "Bored" gave me latitude to call all the shots. "Bored" let me be dreamy to my heart's content. "Why don't you call up Mary Nelle Waters?" she'd suggest. "She's a very nice girl, even though she wears dresses."

Inviting company to play was always a command performance, and I'd answer the doorbell, dragging my feet, a grim hostess indeed. Mary Nelle and I played until we had a falling out, an inevitability because we were both strong-willed girls. She'd get around to laughing at my southern accent and calling me "Mushmouth" and I'd yell, "Damn Yankee!" at her because anyone who pronounced their *i*'s in a crisp, superior, bright-eyed way was a Yankee to a southern child. I could drawl out the word "Yankee" so blasphemously, so lip-curlingly snide that Mary Nelle Waters would cry with shame. Once she took her revenge by setting a paper sack containing a dead squirrel in one of the basement windows. She positioned it behind a curtain so that days passed before we finally located the source of the merciless odor.

Of the children Granny introduced me to, I liked Fayette and Rocky Roo the best. I loved their names; they were feisty kids who went barefooted and liked to chew the skin off tar bubbles, too. They both looked like Huckleberry Finn. But aside from Fayette and Rooky Roo, I pleaded with my grandmother for solitude. "Can't I just poke?" I'd ask her. "It's summertime." The word seemed a verbal talisman I might employ at the mention of a disagreeable invitation. She'd look at me critically, as if into a mirror, then she'd let her face go loose and bright with recognition. "Yes," she'd say, "isn't summer wonderful all by itself?" She'd say this in a secretive way, bunching her shoulders, busying herself once again at her vanity, daubing her

face with Charles of the Ritz Velvet Texture lotion, which made me
think of summer as some kind of vanishing cream one might slather
over blemishes of inconvenience.

I'd watch her take a metal nail file and measure a precise amount of
Chantilly powder onto the tip and sprinkle the powder inside her
brassiere. It was the only scent she liked. If I asked her to, she'd take
out her teeth and let me examine them. She'd sing, "I Went to the
Animal Fair" as many times as I liked. And with tireless, big-eyed ex-
pressiveness, she'd recite rhymes from her childhood:

> Onery, orry, ickery Ann,
> Philistan, Phalistan, Nicholas, Jan
> Oueevy, quavy, English Navy,
> Stinktum, stanktum, cherrico bunk!

She'd allow me to mess with her hearing aids and try on all her
hats with veils. And her eyes would mist fondly as she told me about
growing up in Kentucky and her home, Granite Hill, the estate near
Danville that no longer belonged to the family. She told me lots about
Nannie, her mother, and showed me the elegant tortoise-shell combs
that had once anchored Nannie's braids. She brought out a fan made
from black ostrich plumes and a ladylike parasol that Nannie had carried on her arm to tea parties. She, like my own mother, her daughter,
had gone home every summer to visit until her parents died. She had
taken three children alone in a '34 Chevrolet and driven a thousand
miles down lumpy dirt roads that stretched tenuously between the oil
fields in Oklahoma, where she'd lived, and the farm in Kentucky.
Nothing, she said, would have stopped her.

It wasn't until I was an adult with children of my own, long after both
Granny and Dada had died, that my mother told me the truth about
them. I forget exactly how she told me—only that there was nothing
vicious in her confession. Her truth sprung from a context that had
everything to do with family continuity, but in one startling, inno-

cence-unraveling moment, she revealed to me that my grandparents' marriage had been fraught with despair, that there had been times when Dada's rage had shattered the Fiesta Ware. Granny had taken her children back to Kentucky every summer to escape him.

"In today's world she'd have left him," my mother said. "But it was the Depression. What would she have done? Where would she have gone?"

"Home!" I said. "To Nannie in Kentucky."

"Impossible," my mother said. "Granny's father had taken a grim view of her elopement to begin with. As far as he was concerned, she'd made her bed and she could lie in it."

The mystery I now confronted was not so much the source of my grandparents' incompatibility, what devils my grandfather had wrestled with, or why my grandmother had stuck with him. The mystery that loomed largest of all was my mother's seemingly vibrant tolerance. As she talked about her childhood, it was clear that shadows of her parents' troubles hung over her still. Then how was she able to return, summer after summer, to Mount Vernon to visit them? How had she been able to forgive her parents enough so that she could share her children with them?

Listening to her recall old griefs, I couldn't be swayed. The unhappy parents that belonged to my mother bore no resemblance to the grandparents I had known; I couldn't share my mother's disappointments. I felt eerily unrelated to her. Who was this man who'd been so stingy and glum, this weak and dreamy wife? How were they the same affable, vigorous people I'd clung to and loved, guardians of my happy childhood? Listening to my mother's revelation, I felt voluminous gratitude. That she had allowed me the romance of my grandparents seemed a brave and generous gift, those trips to Mount Vernon and the imperishable memories they brought to my life a kind of counterweight to the burdens she'd borne as a child. Love, despite its flaws and lapses, had been allowed to come full circle.

My mother's decision to take us to Mount Vernon was as much an exercise of her faith in possibility as a gesture toward reconciliation. Our unspoiled, unknowledgeable hearts made us go-betweens of an infectious goodwill. We were unencumbered by the past; watching her parents attend us, my mother must have felt a mixture of relief and wistfulness.

Maybe my grandparents were more receptive in the summertime than at any other time during the year. Our visit was occasion for their release from whatever pinched routines they otherwise obeyed. We commanded their audience; we asked torrential questions; we raised up the ghosts of their pasts and walked fearlessly beside them; we begged them away from the confines of themselves. A breeze poured busily through their house all day, freshening the air with our comings and goings. Curtains twirled at the windows, and no door was ever locked.

When my own children return from a holiday spent with grand-parents, they carry a boxful of treasure: seashell necklaces Papa has fashioned, the glistening hulls of June bugs, sycamore balls, gnarled and squatty mushrooms, the tangible stars of early fallen maple leaves—all things bright and beautiful gathered on a walk in the wild woods with loved ones. They have seen a lizard for the first time. Their pockets bulge with bird feathers, chunks of milky quartz. Their faces bloom with satisfaction.

I think they look taller, looser, older somehow. Are they really as beautiful as they seem to be, or is their beauty a trick of happiness as they troop home with their spoils? For a moment, seeing them, I am my own mother watching my flush-faced play long ago in Mount Vernon. I am my grandmother glimpsing my young mother's face brighten on the drive up the lane of one-hundred-year-old oak trees at Granite Hill. I am Nannie's pioneer-stock mother, shading her eyes, gazing into a field simmering with the ruckus of wildflowers where her children leap and chase and disappear like dreams. I am myself, ten years old, calling after my crazy brothers to Stop! Wait up! as we race to the swimming pool at the London Hall Motor Inn over which dazzles the fiery weather of dreams: stars of a billion summers yet to come, light of a billion summers past just now filtering to Earth.

Help

MY CHILDHOOD TOOK place in a time when you could stand perfectly still and the world delivered itself to you, person by person, with courtesy and efficiency, and frequently attired in a uniform. The milkman drove his chubby little cartoon truck into our driveway two mornings a week and brought us milk, butter, and eggs, which he did not leave on the stoop but carried inside and deposited directly into our refrigerator. Sometimes we were still in our pajamas, eating breakfast in the kitchen. The bottles, clinking in the metal basket the milkman carried, made an opulent sound, like heaps of pocket change. They were voluptuous bottles, molded of sturdy glass, crowned with bright red pleated paper caps that opened like pulling a hem string, loose and zigzag easily. In the milkman's truck, more bottles of milk and cream nested in square metal tubs filled with ice. It was a peculiar sort of ice, not sculpted in cubes or crushed into chips, but packable like soft snow: airy and spongelike and crusty, as if, miraculously, it had been toasted. It melted quickly and tasted lacy, electric, and oddly warm: ice you could chew and drink at the same time. Our mothers said it was dirty, which made it taste all the more delicious. Besides,

there was a saying in my family that you were supposed to eat five
pounds of dirt before you died no matter what. We'd loiter around
the truck, especially in the summertime, begging for scoops of the
stuff, and our milkman always complied.

The postman delivered our mail twice a day. Lane's Laundry
brought my father's shirts folded in square cellophane-wrapped packages. They looked and smelled nearly salty with starch, like large crisp
soda crackers for a giant—that's what I pretended, helping to unwrap
them. Between the pressed shirts were oblongs of cardboard that I
saved to draw on.

Two newspapers arrived—morning and evening editions—even
in a poky little town like ours, delivered by two different paperboys
who rode bikes. Strapped across their chests they carried big white
gunny sacks, dangling and flapping like saddlebags. The paperboys
rode with an extravagant display of mission. They appeared not to
steer their bikes with anything more than willpower, their hands free
to dip into their sacks and sling papers which they had folded with
aerodynamic precision. They were loose and confident riders, but
purposeful, not sloppy, and they had mastered launching the papers
from their sacks to the recipient's front porch with the swift archery of
an arm that hung upon the air after its toss as lyrically as a dancer's.

The Bookmobile, eggplant colored, tortoiselike with its load, lum-
bered around the neighborhood in the summer, offering library
services once a week. The truck garden man parked his fruit-and-
vegetable-laden pickup on the corner of Madison and Beverly every
Friday afternoon. Mostly we bought fresh fruit from him: mushy lo-
cally grown cantaloupes, watermelon, leathery scuppernong grapes,
and soft glowing peaches that smelled like Chanel No. 5 for my
mother's fresh peach pies.

At twilight, the ice cream man materialized on his clown-colored
scooter, ringing a bell. We'd leap up from the dinner table and beg
our parents for nickels and dimes, then scamper into the dusk, hun-
gering after a spectacle of sweetness. It was the sort of giddy other-
worldly food that we imagined we would eat to our heart's content if
we ever ran away from home, frozen confections that weren't sold

widely in grocery stores then. It was the bounty of choice that enthralled us, the near-wickedness of so many flavors and gaudy gypsy
colors beckoning from frosty trays. A shivering smoke unraveled in
the jungle-hot air as we bent over to see and cool our faces. There
were Nutty Buddies, Eskimo pies, Fudgesicles, and Dreamsicles,
which were the color of candlelight inside a pumpkin and tasted
creamily orange. There were Circle K Bars, dressed in wrappers decorated with bowlegged cowboys twirling lassoes, and little tubs of
plain old vanilla and chocolate ice cream that you ate with a flat stubby
wooden spoon, a friendly version of the hateful tongue depressor.
There were Brown Mules and frozen Milky Ways and Zero bars. He
sold Popsicles, of course, in their polka-dot wrappers: cherry, orange,
banana, grape, and on rare occasions the magical blueberry, which was
the astonishing artificial turquoise of swimming pool water and had a
blustery arctic flavor. Once I touched my tongue to a blueberry Popsicle and it stuck. I rode my bike home in a panic to get help, holding
the blistering Popsicle against my tongue all the way; but it wouldn't
melt free until my mother poured water on it.

In and out of the neighborhood wound the city buses, bringing the
maids. We lived in a modest, middle-class neighborhood: a mix of
young doctors, lawyers, postal workers, engineers, businessmen, real
estate brokers, public-school teachers, insurance brokers, and bankers.
The cost of hiring a maid was $5 per day. Most everyone could afford
to hire help one or two days a week—except the help, of course.

The maids who disembarked from the buses that stopped at the
corner of Madison and Beverly ranged in age and comportment, but
they were all women and black. Some arrived decked out in their uniforms; some wore regular dresses and shoes and carried paper sacks
with their uniforms folded inside. They would change clothes in their
employers' utility rooms or in a half-bath that they were allowed to
use. It was thought that they subscribed to a different hygienic code
from whites. They smelled different: of the kerosene with which some

of them heated their houses, of pomade, which flattened or slicked their grizzled hair, of cabbage and other leafy greens cooked in fatback, of Bargain Box clothes and old run-over shoes and bus exhaust and thin dimes and exhaustion.

Our first maid, Etta Williams, was a scrunched-up tar-colored little woman with short, greasy hair that bristled from her head like a rooster's comb. She was so black that even her gums were black; but the soles of her feet and her palms were a satiny valentine pink. Although Mother hired her to clean house and iron, she mostly ended up rocking a squalling baby in her lap or feeding us lunch or mopping up after one of our childish disasters with finger paint or spilled milk. She was married to a retired preacher; there wasn't much money. To earn extra income, Etta would often stay after her regular workday on Friday to feed us supper and to baby-sit while my parents went out. We always complained when she stayed. We liked energetic sitters like Mrs. Baxter, who when she told the story of "Little Red Riding Hood" would take out her false teeth and clack them together when she talked like the wolf. Etta knew no stories. By the end of her long workday, she was so tired that, after washing our supper dishes, all she could manage was to flop herself into the green leatherette armchair in the den, prop her feet on the ottoman, and go to sleep. It was like being baby-sat by a pile of old clothes. My brothers and I liked to spy on her while she slept. We'd drop bits of paper in her hair or take off her slippers and switch them on her feet. We'd tickle her face with a weed or a feather to make her twitch. When she was deeply asleep, you could even raise her eyelids if you dared and watch her sleeping dead eyes. The whites of her eyes were as murky as chocolate milk.

After Etta retired, Mother hired the intimidating Ora Covington, a sullen, moody wall of a woman who kept a little flask in her apron pocket and nipped on it all day long. Her housekeeping skills were matchless, but she would have nothing to do with childcare.

Betty Lane came to work for us when I was in junior high school, and she stayed the longest. Vigorous and lighthearted, chatty, congenial, Betty was a whizbang ironer, and she taught me how to iron a

man's shirt. There wasn't anything slap-dash about the procedure; it was ritualistic and precise, like a cat licking itself. She believed in voodoo, romance, and that eating four-leaf clovers would bring you phenomenal luck. She had a talent for finding four-leaf clovers wherever she stood, and she would pick them and save them for me to eat so that I would never be lovelorn. I knew how much Betty weighed: 165 pounds—astonishing because she was so short and compactly built. "It's all muscle," she'd say. She drank eight glasses of water a day for the health of her complexion. Her skin was taut and unblemished, a sunny butterscotch color. I knew her daughters' names and ages, what their aspirations were and who had asthma attacks. I knew that she was married to a good man named Paul who ran a body shop out of their garage. They lived in the country and raised hogs to eat. They lived near a road where a pot of turnip greens had been hexed by a witch doctor and left for a neighbor to eat. After he'd eaten them, sure enough he'd taken sick and died. I was in college by the time Betty quit working for my family. Her oldest daughter, Georgia Mae, was college-bound herself and Betty had learned that she could make more money cleaning offices at Gilbarco Corporation than cleaning for my mother.

This was the last era of affordable help for the middle class, a time, too, of service with a smile, of bag boys wheeling out cartloads of groceries and unloading them into your trunk for tips, of men who routinely pumped gas and washed windshields while we relaxed inside our cars, listening to the radio, of doctors making house calls, hastening to the sickbeds of rich and poor alike. I remember riding with my father to make such a visit to a little tin shack that looked like a coffee pot. The weeds in the yard stood hip high. The shack had a rusty spout for a chimney and smoke huffed raggedly in the cold blue air above the roof. An old white woman lived in the shack, a widow, who paid my father from a fat roll of cash that she unfurled from her bathrobe pocket. A house call in those days cost $7 (an office visit cost $5). If you were a young doctor hoping to enlarge your practice, you often accepted facsimiles of payment: farm eggs, a cured ham, a bushel of corn, yard work, a purebred puppy in trade. Sometimes people couldn't pay my father anything, but he went out to their houses anyway. He said he was obliged to do so by his Hippocratic oath.

If my mother was feeling beleaguered by children, if she couldn't shoo us away to plunder some other mother's patience for a while, if she simply didn't feel like piling us all in the car for a trip to the grocery store, she phoned in a grocery order at one of several markets in town that offered delivery service. I remember listening to her specify a pound of bacon, "lean," a head of lettuce, "firm," a loaf of bread, "fresh." You had to be explicit or the grocer might deliver inferior goods.

Even as we slept, the world continued to breeze in and out of our lives as if through an invisible revolving door. At sunrise, garbage collectors walked through our yard to the back porch to fetch our trashcans, heft them to the street, empty and return them to the porch and place their lids tightly back on. The street-cleaning machine swished along our summer-radiant streets, dampening the dust with a fine mist of water that made the air smell limp and rainy. In the spring, somebody's maid could usually refer us to a relative who would till up kitchen gardens or lime and reseed lawns. Sometimes they'd bring a mule and we children would sit on the curb all day, watching the mule plow, yearning to befriend it. We were not so much spoiled as enabled to get on with our lives in productive and imaginative ways because of such help.

There were men who came around regularly, looking to paint or to clean gutters or wash windows. Only once did somebody mistakenly hire an escaped convict. But the convict did the work asked of him and moved discreetly on. In his wake there arrived a Lions Club member selling sturdy mops and brooms, handmade by the blind, or an encyclopedia salesman, a Mormon missionary, or the skinny little weasel-faced man who sold toilet-bowl cleaners. My parents always invited him inside because he was so earnestly polite and they felt sorry for him. He was down on his luck, had a sick wife—my father made it his business to listen to everybody's story.

When my parents invited people who were selling things into our home, they did so graciously. There was never a sense that they felt interrupted or intruded upon. Everybody had good manners; the salespeople had good manners and we children had good manners, too. It was an opportunity for everybody to practice courtesy and to exercise good manners, whether there would be an exchange of money for products or not. We learned firsthand what a fish handshake was and why you didn't use one.

These door-to-door exchanges were vivid and energetic connections. They occurred on porches, or inside hallways or foyers if the weather was rainy or cold. People looked one another in the eye without suspicion. There was a feeling of shoulder-to-shoulder heaving ho, of attention to minor details, of common cause, of decent well-meaning strangers affecting our welfare, of folks pitching in to ensure not only their own livelihoods but reliable service to a broad number of people.

If this childhood sounds too privileged, too protected and dreamy, remember that the A-bomb hovered in the background. We knew from reading our *Weekly Reader*s about its detonated mushroom shape, an arrowhead tipped in poison. Air-raid sirens wailed at noon on Saturdays, testing, testing. Public schools conducted evacuation practices and people built bomb-shelters lined with lead walls and stocked with water and provisions in serious preparation for nuclear war.

It was a time, too, when American children suffered more from disease than depression; there were no vaccines against measles, mumps, or chicken pox. The specter of whooping cough flapped over my bed in the dark, a grim version of the cranes and storks who delivered babies. The word *dysfunction* had yet to be apprehended and marshaled into service for explaining aberrations of human behavior. Adults had nervous breakdowns, but children were spared such afflictions; our battle was with the invisible polio virus. It lurked in the shadows of every playground, floated upon the surfaces of public swimming pools, infiltrated the mouthpieces of drinking fountains, attached itself to the handlebars of stray bicycles, skate keys, sand buckets, toys, chain-link fences. In the blazing summertime lull of our mandatory naps, we children listened for the polio cars to cruise past, patrolling the streets. The cars were lean and black, with toothy grilles like sharks. On their roofs perched cloverleaves of megaphone-style speakers, proclaiming in booming doomsday voices the dangers of exposure to the virus and cautioning children to rest. The polio cars looked driverless or, worse, driven by the ghosts of polio victims. In the heat of my bedroom, my skin pocked with impressions of chenille, I shivered thinking of the slithering cars, frightening myself away from the very nap that might save me. The cars circled stealthily. They seemed to be looking for somebody not paying attention, not heeding their warnings, a child they might arrest.

My mother doesn't remember these cars and says I must have imagined them. But I did not imagine them or their cautionary surveillance: IT'S POLIO SEASON AND ALL CHILDREN NEED TO REST. CALLING ALL CHILDREN, CALLING ALL CHILDREN, GET INTO YOUR BEDS FOR NAPS. The messages were like rounds of thunder you wanted to hide from; but in some strange way I found them reassuring—one more indication that the world beyond my parents' jurisdiction was ultimately beneficent, populated by unknown legions of humane and sensible people working to protect me from disease.

By 1954, multitudes of children victoriously alive and still unknotted by paralysis would line up in school cafeterias and auditoriums and libraries to be vaccinated against future chances of infection. My grandfather, by then a retired public health officer, would assist in vaccinating the student body of Sternberger Elementary School. For me the dread of the shot would be tempered by his stolid presence, but also by the notion I had then of the world's steadfast goodwill. Even the evening television news, as reported by Douglas Edwards, was so gray and nonthreatening it could put a child to sleep. What a blessing it was to learn that certain scientists had dedicated entire careers to preventing polio in children they would never meet, that once again help was being offered by people we didn't know, trustworthy strangers devoted to improving our lives. It was still safe for children to take gifts from strangers and not yet unwise for them to leave the doors of their hearts unlocked.

The Yellow Rose

EVERY EVENING, ARRIVING home from his office or the hospital, my
father swooped my mother into his arms and softened her up with a
kiss. She'd grown prickly in the desert of his absence, tending us children all day. It was a juicy, watering hole of a kiss—you could hear it
from any room in our house. He had a wide, plush mouth and no
shame whatsoever, and he might have gobbled my mother right up
where she stood cooking French fries or mashing potatoes had there
been no small children underfoot, tugging at his pants leg, pulling his
stethoscope out of his pocket, making whatever racket we could to
gain access, to peel them apart. We could not have been more intrusive
had we been skunks.

My parents had met in Dallas, Texas, in November, 1945, and the
story handed down to us kids was that Mother had been so immediately smitten that she came in from their blind date, summoned all
her roommates to bear witness, announced that she'd met the man she
would marry, then stood on her head. On their second date, my father proposed to her, and less than three months later, they married—
the day after Valentine's, 1946.

From my child's perspective, a bold, compulsive, publicly demonstrative passion distinguished my parents' marriage. Certainly romantic urgency had been at the heart of their courtship and wedding; but even after we children began to crowd and pester them, they never lost center stage with one another.

They went out to parties often. They took weekend vacations without us—to golfing resorts, mostly. They attended dinner dances, my father fretfully attired in a tuxedo, the bib and tie and cummerbund of which gave him such trouble that my mother always intervened. That he relied upon her to finish dressing him, to uncomplicate whatever he bungled or didn't understand, gave her an aura of competence that we children relied upon. He was the worker in the family, but Mother was the fixer, the mechanic and fine finisher. She stood by his side, matchlessly serene, wearing her emerald taffeta strapless evening gown, a sheath as slender as a blade of grass. She'd corralled three children for early baths, cooked and fed us supper, untangled our father from his tuxedo, and she emerged from such tumult and squalor without one hair askew, without a wrinkle in the chic green gown.

I loved my mother in a needy, starveling's way. My brothers did, too. We couldn't get enough of her. We competed with one another for her attention, and we competed with our father. We begrudged her long conversations with friends on the telephone. We'd lie on the bed beside her, twitchy with impatience, eavesdropping in plain view, waiting for her to hang up. It seemed we were stuck, unable to fully dramatize our lives without her approving audience. We depended on her spark, her ease, her companionable laughter, the compassion in her soft brown gaze. I swooned after the fragrances that trailed her: Lustre Creme shampoo, Moon Drops cold cream, Jergens almond-scented hand lotion, the ornate, operatic bouquet of L'Aire du Temps perfume. The latticework of those smells clung to the fabric of her nightgown along with the chirpy aroma of the bacon she fried us every morning, the secretive singed smell of her Chesterfield cigarettes mingling with the sweet cool vapor of her Doublemint breath.

She was everybody's friend and confidante, her heart a repository, a haven for the messy, complex matters of our childhood. She was an ardent listener. She thought we were all much funnier than we were. She savored our naive philosophies and responded with thoughtful and sober attention. She endured our follies and exploits, indulged our swagger with unwavering fascination, burying her mind in our evolution like a student rapt in deciphering illuminated manuscripts.

At no time was my mother more exalted than at Christmas. Our whole family scrambled around her like elves, trying to please. She was fun to please because she expressed her gratitude so flamboyantly. She could take a child's little molehill gift and, lifting it from its box, transform it into Mount Everest.

Ritually, the last gift she opened on Christmas Day was our father's. Too ostentatious to have been set under the tree (it would have made the other presents look shabby), he fetched it with much fanfare from the attic or a closet. The gift tended to be something my father couldn't easily afford, wrapped thickly in Montaldo's signature holiday papers, either dazzling metallic red or green. The bow seemed the truest prize, so artfully posh that I saved it and draped it around my neck to wear as a medallion, days afterward.

Beneath their flashing wrappings, the Montaldo's boxes were a slippery dolphin gray, deep enough to hold whole ensembles of clothes. Traditionally, when she glimpsed their gorgeous and surprising contents, my mother collapsed into tears. It wasn't Christmas unless she cried. She lifted the silky garments from their basinets of tissue into the light of Christmas Day with an expression of trembling reverence. She nuzzled them, inhaled their worldly fragrances, waltzed them around the room as the tears spilled down her cheeks. We children gathered around, stroking her. "Don't cry, Mommy," we implored. But there was something magical and inspiring about tears overflowing the wellspring of delight. Our revelation that happiness had a mature and tender side—the opposite from ticklish and silly— expanded its repertoire. To watch our mother smiling through her tears was to witness the sort of paradox that inclined us to believe powerfully in the ultimate triumph of gladness over sorrow.

Once Daddy gave her a little squirrel stole; another year, a dress designed by Molly Parnis, who outfitted Mamie Eisenhower. One Christmas he gave her an emerald-cut diamond on a silver, thread-thin chain, and there was the morning she opened the smoke-colored beaver jacket and cried over it for nearly an hour. Each gift was impeccably tasteful—the salesladies at Montaldo's took Daddy carefully under their wings. They were the sorts of gifts my mother would have never lavished upon herself. Her own father had been a cheapskate—she recalled that during the Great Depression she'd owned two school dresses, a pink one and a green one, which she alternated daily. It's conceivable that my mother wept when she opened Daddy's grandiose boxes because her luck had so overwhelmingly changed. Perhaps she cried for all the women still living with cheapskates. How had she managed to attach herself to such a generous man?

I tried to imagine a gift that would make me cry, but I couldn't. Maybe a horse. Was it because we children were accustomed to generosity and had never done without? Because of her stingy upbringing, my mother didn't take largesse for granted.

My father bumbled around in front of her tears. "Don't you *like* the dress, Bunny?" he'd say, perplexed. She'd laugh as she blotted her eyes. "I *love* the dress, Rod. You know I do. But it's too much. All I gave you was a boring old shirt." And her observance of the inequity usually triggered a fresh onslaught of tears.

My father's reward was in knowing that he was the champion giver of gifts. It was his immutable status within our family.

Maybe his extravagance made my mother feel too much like a child, her ability to reciprocate in kind, dwarfed. Perhaps, in some way she couldn't articulate, my father's gifts made her feel beholden. How might she live up to his queenly expectations of her? He thought he was being appropriately worshipful. He courted her anew over the packages she opened. There was a ritualistic dance they performed of hesitancy and disapproval. Why had he spent so much? Why did Christmas turn him into such a boy? No matter how vigorous her protests, she couldn't shrink his capacious heart. If he stood mildly by, looking dumbfounded long enough, she'd rise above her uncertainties and chastisements and sink herself against him in an embrace that sundered anyone's doubts about her not being the happiest woman in the world.

There came a time, however, when she was not so happy. Daddy's practice was thriving and perhaps she no longer felt part of the struggle they'd shared when he first opened his office in a rented ramshackle wood-frame house with a dirt parking lot on Price Street. Now my mother was housebound, anchored to babies. She complained bitterly whenever Daddy played golf on his day off and stayed at the clubhouse for a cocktail that would make him late to dinner. When he finally arrived, she'd remove his plate from the warming oven, plunk it in front of him, and hasten with a strident silence out of the kitchen. The food, overheated, looked like rigor mortis had set in. "Daddy's in the doghouse," he'd say, glimpsing me peeking at him shyly from the threshold.

He was seldom at home in the evenings. If he wasn't on call for emergencies, he went back to his office to update his charts. Assiduous about detailing patient histories, and because his secretary couldn't keep up with the drawling volume of his dictations, he tended to the task himself.

My mother was bound to have felt threatened by the allure of my father's work. It was not simply a career or a calling to him, it was a complete and satisfying seduction, a consummation. Did he seem too satisfied apart from her? There began, too, about this time, the parade of new cars, symbols not only of his economic advancement but also of his boyishly extreme enjoyment of that status. What he regarded as entitlement, or as reward for his hard work, my mother viewed as indulgence, as spendthriftery. My grandfathers had always paid cash for their cars, but my father didn't mind sinking flashily into debt. It would remain the pattern of a lifetime, his bringing home a new car every two or three years. Usually he would select a Buick or a

Chevrolet—although there was a smattering of Plymouths. The smallest car he ever bought was a Valiant, and the largest, a true luxury car, was an Electra with innovative electric windows and locks. The Electra filled our little driveway like a docked cruise ship, and after my mother saw it, she didn't speak to my father for a week. She could get so feisty over a new car gleaming outside, awaiting her inspection, that she looked hot to the touch. "But we don't *need* a new car," she'd seethe. She would rather have had decent furniture for the living room, new rugs, a trip to New York City to see *The King and I*.

One night, late, I thought I heard my parents arguing. Daddy had returned from the hospital after we children were in bed, but I had never fallen asleep. Some nights when I felt restless, I'd trampoline on my bed for a while and practice flipping somersaults. The voices I heard bore no resemblance to my parents'. They sounded shrill, desperate and panic-stricken, like the shouting of people on a leaking ship. "You're not being reasonable," the man said. "Where would you go?" "To Mother's," the woman replied. "I'll take the children and we'll go to Mother's." The firmness of her decisiveness shocked me. Her voice sounded eerily tearless. But the argument boomed from the den where my mother watched her melodramas, and so I reassured myself that what I'd overheard was the overwrought dialogue of actors on TV, not my parents.

Not long afterward, sitting at the kitchen table and eating lunch with her, I caught my mother moping. She looked dulled by disappointment, the expression on her face distinctly drifting toward sorrow. She drummed her fingernails in abstract rhythm on the tabletop while she stared past me out the window into a thinness of expectations. She didn't *see* anything; when a car passed, her eyes didn't follow it. I tried to make conversation. "Why are all the songs on the radio about love?" I asked.

"Are they?"

"Yes. Isn't it dumb?"

"What else should songs be about?" she said, dragging herself out of her trance. "What else is more important?" Her voice turned sharp and defensive and as freighted with lament as the actors'.

꙳

It was during this palpable phase of my mother's displeasure with my father, her playing proctor to his bad boy, that I embarked upon my plan to be the person that Christmas who would give her the single present that would make her cry. Clearly my father had lost favor. I was not the perfect daughter by a long stretch, but I'd never let a clubhouse cocktail come between me and dinner, nor had I foisted upon her an unwanted automobile.

I must have been around nine years old, still too young to ride a city bus downtown to shop by myself. I remember Grandmother Ruth accompanying me to buy Mother's gift at Ellis-Stone department store on Elm Street. I wore my good winter coat over a dress and my white cotton church gloves. Those were the days when proper southern ladies dressed up to shop downtown. My grandmother wore a prim gray suit, fashionable pumps with stout heels (not the spike heels my mother was fond of), a gray hat with a fluff of veil, and pearl ear-bobs. Christmas decorations entwined every streetlamp. Salvation Army bells unfurled sparkles of sound upon the chilly air; I pretended it was music shaken loose from a reindeer's harness. I felt like skipping across the crosswalks, but my grandmother clamped my hand firmly in her own, and we marched along to her stern, protective beat.

Ellis-Stone was the store where Mother bought our shoes. The shoe department operated a fluoroscope machine where you could see ghoulish green x-rays of your spindly toe bones inside new shoes and determine if you had a proper fit. Near the cashier's counter, a mechanical palomino horse outfitted with soft grimy leather reins stood ready to buck you around for a dime. I wanted to patronize Ellis-Stone not only because my mother approved of shopping there, but because it was where I'd seen the tiara. I'd determined to buy my mother a rhinestone tiara for Christmas because she was the Queen and because I knew she'd let me borrow it whenever I felt like dressing up. It was a splendid crown of jewels, almost holy, like a halo. Whenever I played Monopoly and landed on LUXURY TAX, I thought of the tiara.

I'd told my taciturn grandmother about the tiara and she'd agreed to escort me downtown to buy it; she'd offered neither an opinion nor enthusiasm. I believed that she secretly wanted the tiara for herself and was jealous that I'd planned to give it to Mother. At heart, Grandmother Ruth was a Victorian, a former one-room-schoolhouse teacher, a knuckle-rapper, a prohibitionist, humorless and bossy. She sulked if you beat her at card games. My mother dyed her hair the lively honey blonde of our cocker spaniel and she smoked cigarettes. She'd been an airline stewardess when she met and impetuously married my father. She was fond of saying—and didn't mind if Grandmother overheard—that if she hadn't fallen in love with Daddy, her ambition had been to sing torch songs in nightclubs.

I tugged loose from my grandmother's grip, scampered across an expanse of snow-colored marble, and entered Ellis-Stone through a heavy glass door. I made a beeline for the glass jewelry case where I'd seen the tiara. Alas, the beautiful crown of wishing stars had ascended, levitated from its earthly perch on black velvet and floated away to make somebody else's dreams come true. "Sold," the saleslady confirmed, and although she showed me a simpler, child-size version, I remained nearly inconsolable. It seemed as if the entire fate of the world had shifted dramatically, as it would have had there been no Wise Men bearing their precious, inimitable gifts.

Grandmother Ruth was quick to point out an array of pins constructed of rhinestones: the prettiest was shaped like a snowflake. But I knew that my mother wasn't a pin person, or a bracelet person for that matter. Bracelets would manacle her busy hands, and get in the way when she did dishes. Pins were sedate old-lady jewelry. Fairy tale queens and princesses wore crowns and necklaces and glass slippers, not pins. Perhaps, in pointing them out, my grandmother was thinking of something *she'd* like for Christmas.

"Could I interest you in pearls?" inquired the saleslady.

I shook my head vehemently. Only rhinestones would do. Then I saw the necklace. I hadn't noticed it because it was out of the case, draping the neck of a plastic torso. Rhinestones dribbled in all directions, bejeweling the mannequin's collarbones. There were three strands of rhinestones from which dangled larger, pear-shaped stones. The effect was that of an elaborate constellation caught in a spider's web. "That's the one," I said.

The saleslady hesitated. "It's very showy," she said, glancing at my grandmother for reinforcement. "Does the lady you're buying this for go to evening parties? Dances?"

"Often enough," said my grandmother tersely. I could tell that she thought the saleslady was being nosy.

The saleslady began to unfasten the necklace from the display. I observed what a complicated process it was because the delicate separate strands kept tangling. Finally she arranged the necklace on a bed of cotton inside a flat white box and gift-wrapped it. "That will be $2.98," she said. It was all the money I had in the world.

Afterward, to celebrate, Grandmother Ruth took me to the S & W Cafeteria and allowed me to eat two chocolate puddings for dessert and the sugar-loaded orange drink (instead of milk) that my mother never bought me. Howard Waynick, who was a neighbor of my grandmother's, played the organ there on the balcony above the lobby. As soon as we'd eaten lunch, we walked over to speak to Howard and my grandmother requested "Winter Wonderland," which Howard played jauntily. Afterward, he gave me his autograph on a napkin.

On Christmas Eve, my father left work early to shop. He had a few traditions of his own that he didn't rely upon my mother to sustain. He bought a couple of cartons of fresh eggnog at the grocery. He bought a few fifths of Jack Daniel's whiskey at the ABC store to distribute to some of his doctor friends. If a patient hadn't already given him a fruitcake, he went out and obtained one. It was food nobody in our family would eat, except Daddy. Even new fruitcake looked old and leftover. The petrified fruit was as hard as marbles. Daddy said there was a trick to eating it. If you dunked it in eggnog, it was delicious, he said, and we were all really missing something if we didn't try it. Fruitcake looked like a loaf of baked dogfood to me.

Off he went on his secret errands, which included a ritual stop at Montaldo's, on Christmas Eve, mind you, without a clue in his head about what Mother wanted. He preferred giving gifts that weren't needed, or wanted, that were total surprises, that nobody would have thought to ask for. He relied on the taste of the matronly staff and on his weak judgment of what Mother would look good wearing, or the sorts of clothes he'd like to see her wearing—which tended toward the provocative: low necklines, slits in skirts. He liked showing her off. Fortunately, the majority of clothing sold in Montaldo's in the early 1950s tended to be decorous and prim, what a rich pilgrim on the cutting edge of fashion might have worn.

This particular Christmas Eve, he motioned me aside and asked if I'd accompany him. The invitation was an astonishing breach in tradition. Nobody was supposed to know what Mother's gift was until she opened it. "We'll listen to Christmas carols on the radio," he cajoled. "Come on, Punky, ride with me so I won't be lonesome."

I should have guessed that he was charting new, uncertain territory on this trip. We didn't drive in the direction of Montaldo's at all. We stopped instead at Harvey West Music Company, and I followed him inside to the record department. "I'd like to by a copy of 'The Yellow Rose of Texas,'" he told the clerk, but they'd sold out.

We left and drove to Moore Music Store, then to a place in south Greensboro near Hamburger Square, where the bums slept under newspapers. I wasn't allowed to go with my friends to the National Theatre in south Greensboro, even though we all hankered to. They showed only horror movies there and the black people in the balcony, which was where they were required to sit, poured their soft drinks and popcorn on your head on purpose—at least this was the rumor.

I liked strolling down the sidewalk in south Greensboro with my tall, cheerful father. It wasn't the menacing place I'd been told it was at all. Between the parking lot and the store where we were headed, my father ran into at least three patients and enjoyed friendly conversations. By the time we arrived at the music store, it seemed like an incidental stop. They didn't have one copy of "The Yellow Rose of Texas" in the place.

"Maybe we ought to give up," I suggested.

"Oh, we'll find it somewhere," he said, marching up the street toward Woolworth's. Snow flurried around us. I remember thinking that his perseverance had something to do with the snowflakes spinning miraculously down from the sky. We never had a white Christmas, but suddenly there was the possibility of one. We loped north on Elm Street toward less seedy shops. We couldn't get half a block without my father running into somebody he knew. He seemed taller and gladder than anyone, shaking hands. His birthday was February 12, Abe Lincoln's birthday, and striding along beside him I could believe my father was somebody famous, too. He was the embodiment of a robust goodwill, and I felt its warm contagion, keeping company with him on the street. I felt on the verge of reward. And finally, in Woolworth's, we located a single 45-rpm recording of Mitch Miller's rendition of "The Yellow Rose of Texas" that we'd first heard on *Your Hit Parade*.

"Don't we have to shop for a record player now, so she'll be able to play it?" I asked him after he'd paid for the record. It cost 97 cents. My parents didn't own a record player, but he shrugged.

"I'm not buying it for her to play," my father said.

Of course he'd never mentioned during our excursion that he was shopping for Mother. Why had I assumed it? He was the one who admired "The Yellow Rose of Texas," not Mother. He loved all uptempo ballad-type songs, rousing gospel, Sousa marches, alma maters, themes from popular movies, and cowboy tunes, music that glorified bravery and sentiment. Whenever "The Yellow Rose of Texas" played on the radio, he'd tap his foot to its beat and grin and tell my mother that it was *their* song, that she was his yellow rose. What was she to do with such a cornball? She'd flip the dial on the radio, dousing his sentimentality with the sophisticated music she preferred: Rosemary Clooney, Judy Garland, Dinah Shore, Frank Sinatra, Perry Como, Julius LaRosa, Nat King Cole.

The pioneer spirit was very much the rage in the early 1950s. My brothers had asked Santa to bring them Davy Crockett–style coonskin caps. James Arness had premiered as Matt Dillon in television's

first adult western, *Gunsmoke*. John Wayne was a leading box office
star. "Cattle Call," sung by Eddie Arnold, was a hit single, along with
Mitch Miller's "Yellow Rose of Texas."

But my mother wasn't a cowgirl. She didn't sing along with "The
Yellow Rose of Texas" like she sang along with Patti Page crooning
"The Tennessee Waltz." She liked sad, heartbroken tunes. If Daddy
thought his record was the sort of gift that would make her weep with
joy, I figured he'd set himself up for disappointment—if, indeed, the
record was for her. It didn't seem at all like my father to spend Christmas Eve shopping for himself. What did it mean, if he was giving her
a record that she couldn't play? It meant a lucky break for me and my
fabulous rhinestone necklace. Clearly, I'd won our competition, and
riding along in our warm car on Christmas Eve, my father whistling
with larky confidence, victorious in his purchase, I felt a little sorry
for him.

On Christmas morning, everybody in our family—except Grandmother Ruth and Granddaddy—ate breakfast in their pajamas. We
didn't even bother to comb our hair. It was Grandmother Ruth who
insisted that, after breakfast, teeth had to be brushed, beds made,
dishes done, before the first present could be opened. Of course we all
howled with protest—even Daddy.

Our ritual for opening presents was to gather around the Christmas tree and wait for Daddy to read the tags, one at a time. If your
name was called, you opened your present while everyone watched.
You passed the present around to be examined and exclaimed over.
Nobody dove in and opened their loot in a rush. It was a slow, methodical, infuriating process of observation, mostly. The slowest gifts
were the ones Daddy opened from patients: boring gifts like golf tees
or highball glasses. There was the occasional adult gift with a private
joke behind it, given by some wisecracking friend, like the set of pillowcases my mother opened one year. On one side of each pillowcase
there was a little rabbit in a sombrero; embroidered beneath him was

YES. On the other side of the pillowcase, the rabbit was lying down and snoozing under his sombrero and the word embroidered under him was NO. My mother and father laughed and winked at one another and tucked the pillowcases back in the box before my grandparents could ask to see them.

That Christmas my parents gave me a record player and the records I'd asked for: "The Nutcracker," "Peter and the Wolf," and "The Peer Gynt Suite"—suggestions from my piano teacher, Mrs. Lake. I also received a new Ginny doll, a baton, and several Nancy Drew mysteries. There were the obligatory clothes from grandparents: a new flannel nightgown, bedroom shoes, a crinoline, a fancy church dress. The pile beneath the tree began to dwindle.

My brothers opened football helmets and shoulder pads, puzzles, Lincoln Logs, cap guns, Mickey Mouse watches, and coonskin caps. My father received mostly socks and shirts and ties. This may have been the Christmas I was reduced, after buying my mother's necklace, to giving him a box of Chiclets. No matter; he acted thrilled, and he slid them into his bathrobe pocket as if to suggest that he would want to chew one soon so would keep them close at hand. My grandparents opened a dull assortment of blankets and towel sets, a new toaster. There were interruptive phone calls all morning—from distant aunts and uncles and my grandparents who lived in Illinois—that waylaid our progress, and by noon, when every kid in the neighborhood was already outside testing a new bike or Flexible Flyer or roller skates, our opening ritual began to feel like a chore. Friends would phone, incredulous that we weren't finished opening. "You're not done? You're kidding! It's one o'clock!" And on we labored, fortified by cups of eggnog that Daddy poured.

Finally, only two presents remained under the tree; a flat parcel containing "The Yellow Rose of Texas" and my gift, wrapped expertly in silver with a blue bow by the professional Ellis-Stone gift-wrapping department. "Why don't you open Marianne's next," Daddy suggested. "'For Mommy,'" he said, reading the card.

"What lovely paper," my mother said appreciatively. I stood close to her, watching her fingers gently split the taped seams of the paper. My heart felt zithery, anticipating her delight. "What a nice, sturdy box," she said with admiration as she carefully lifted the lid. On a pristine bed of cotton, in a glittering tangle, lay the necklace. No telling how many times my brother Knothead had shaken the box, trying to guess what was inside it. "Oh my goodness gracious!" exclaimed my mother.

"You can't even tell what it is until I untangle it," I told her.

"But of course I know what it is!" she said. "It's the sun and the moon and the entire Milky Way all in one. It's jewels fit for a king."

"A queen," I said. "It's to be worn only on special occasions."

"Well, then, let me put it on right now."

"It will make you look rich."

"I'm already rich," she said, pulling me into her arms. We fiddled with the necklace and got it straightened out. I fastened it around her neck, even though she was still wearing her frumpy bathrobe. "How do I look?"

"Beautiful," everyone cooed, and my Mother hugged me close and kissed me and told me over and over how much she loved the necklace—but she didn't cry.

When she opened "The Yellow Rose of Texas," she cried. She held it for a long time, as if absorbing its tune and lyrics by telepathy. She rolled the record slowly between her hands, considerately, meditatively. I didn't know why such a gift would make her cry, didn't understand its magical unplayable declaration. I only understood that my parents communicated on some level of intimacy that I would never be privy to.

"For goodness sake, it's Christmas Day!" Grandmother Ruth said. My mother's tears embarrassed her. "What a mess," she said, bustling out of her chair to gather up the torn paper leavings of our celebration. She could never sit still for long; she was like a human pogo stick.

"Not just yet, Mother," my father said to her, "there's one more gift." Then he took my mother's hands and led her into the entrance hall where a new mahogany hi-fi stood gleaming. Inside its cabinet were stacked a half-dozen record albums by the popular musicians my mother admired. And although she was thrilled with the gift and sang its praises and kissed my father a million times, I saw that the gift didn't equal the little corny record he'd given her earlier, the record which dismantled whatever fences over the past months my mother had thrown up to part herself from him. And he was right; she never played "The Yellow Rose." It was a keepsake, a souvenir that she tucked away. I never saw it again, but it played indelibly in the air, inaudible, inexhaustible, all the days of their lives.

In time I would learn that the necklace I'd given my mother was gaudy, not her style at all, a cheap floozy's adornment. My mother and I would reminisce about the gift and what a tender little girl I'd been and how she'd treasured the necklace in spite of the fact that she never wore it in public. One time, for my sake, she'd pretended to. That same holiday, on the evening of the Century Club Christmas Dance, accompanied by my father trussed up in his tuxedo, my mother left wearing her strapless green ball gown and the twinkling rhinestone necklace. Her neck and shoulders looked wreathed in a galaxy of light. I stood waving goodbye at the window. I never knew, until I was grown, that after she'd settled herself inside the dark car, she carefully removed the necklace and replaced it with her wedding pearls.

In my mind, the necklace had transformed my mother. I was watching the ascent of a star. All the men would line up to dance with her. Their wives would covet the necklace and beg to borrow it. My parents would drink champagne out of glass slippers, and when they danced, all eyes would be cast admiringly upon them. Hero and heroine of a true-life love story, they would float above the dance floor, airborne, dream-borne, far above the mortal and the picayune.

Melissa's Shot

THE SYMPTOMS WERE quickly identifiable as strep throat: swollen glands, fever, listlessness, the telltale white spots dappling the back of a throat so sore it felt like your tonsils had skidded on asphalt. And there was never any question, once the tongue depressor had been snapped decisively in two, what the punishment would be. It was punishment, not treatment, when your physician father was in charge.

He hated for any of us to get sick. *He* never got sick, and there we were, whiny weakling lesser things—*puny* was his word for us. The silence, after the thermometer had been swabbed with disinfectant and returned to the medicine cabinet, was dreadful preparation. You'd pray that the hospital would call with an emergency. You flattened yourself to the bed, so pale and puny that maybe he would mistake you for a sheet.

Inevitably you heard him rummaging in the kitchen for a pot. He never cooked, never even heated water for a cup of instant coffee. What did he want with a pot? You prayed you'd misheard and it was your mother taking the kettle out to heat water for hot tea that she would serve you alongside a plate of buttered toast. She'd straighten your covers, plump up your pillows, sit on the edge of your sickbed while you ate from a tray, indulged like a princess, radiant, wearing your fever like a crown.

Instead, there was that slamming, bumfuddled sound of impatience in the kitchen that your mother never made. Where was that damn pot? And once it was located, you detected the distant tremor of his irritation, his huffing and puffing over the ordeal of finding and needing the pot at all. After all, the pot was slowing him down, impeding his progress in leaving for the hospital. He grumbled to himself as if he were hefting an anchor, not a pudgy little pot. He had twenty or thirty truly sick people to see, and nobody was supposed to get sick in his own family. It was a rule, sort of. He depended on our home as a haven of wellness. That was why we rarely had on hand the ordinary first-aid supplies stocked by other families. No Band-Aids at the ready. No Q-Tips, gauze, Vap-O-Rub, Calamine lotion, Bactine, Mercurochrome, or nose drops. If we kept such things, my goodness, we might *need* them!

With a splattering burst of tap water, he began to fill the pot, banging it against the faucet. It was an aluminum pot, a dull drudgery gray with a heavily dimpled bottom. When it was nearly full, he slapped it onto the burner of our electric stove. You could feel the venomous heat unfurling through the coils. The silence was as dreadful as a poised fang, and then you finally heard a squabbly hissing, the squirmy, puckering sound of water bubbling at full-speed. You heard the terse unhasping of medical bag clasps, brisk delving, snappish closure, then the delicate tink-tink of the glass syringe tumbling in the hot water, tapping out its steamy little polka of hurt, the pot transformed into a makeshift sterilizer for the device that would deliver a jolt of healing penicillin.

Wordlessly, in he marched, the syringe held upright, the needle glistening, elongating as he neared, serum bejeweling the tip, the entire apparatus modeled mercilessly on the bee. It was his no-nonsense delivery that shocked, his dispassionate speed. He might just as well have been a teacher hastily plugging a thumbtack into a bulletin board. Preceding the shot by two seconds was the pungent, cold-hearted aroma of an isopropyl-soaked cotton ball followed by its chilly swipe of wetness on your rump. Then the stinging prick and transfusion of bully medicine. It felt like a pummeling. There was no ceremony, no cajoling, just the unspoken mandate that you roll over and submit.

That my brother Knothead pretended he *liked* shots, would jut out his arm and beg our father to boil the syringe, made my cowardice all the more profound, although it paled beside my younger cousin Melissa's. Once when we were visiting our grandparents in Mt. Vernon, Melissa succumbed to strep throat. She'd never lived in the house of a doctor, knew nothing of the warning sounds: the tiny tympani of a boiling syringe. When my father entered the room where she was resting and she saw the shot barging toward her, unannounced, she emitted a scream of betrayal that was probably heard down at the local police station, and she bolted. The adults had to chase her down. My father and mother, my aunt and uncle raced her through the house and out into the yard. You might have thought she was carrying the Golden Goose. I saw her leap the hammock like a horse in a steeplechase. "Godblessit!" my father yelled as he tripped over a croquet wicket. They kept after her, circling the house, streaking into and through it again, out the front door and down North 12th Street, up somebody's driveway, down the alley with its clutter of trashcans. My granny ambled onto the porch to observe with her binoculars, the way she watched birds. They finally cornered Melissa in the garage where my grandfather parked his blue Imperial and hauled her, wailing, inside. It took three of them to hold her still so my father could stick her.

I'd watched the entire escapade from a blissed-out perch in the sugar maple tree beside the garage, cheering her on as she galloped past, her blonde hair flowing. She was a wild palomino carrying an outlaw self while the thunderous sheriff's posse closed in.

I knew that even as Melissa outran them, she would lose the race. I anticipated her arrest not because she was a frightened, puny kid, but because deep down in her little shock absorber heart, she knew what all beloved kids knew: a posse's job wasn't just to break our will, to round us up for taming; ultimately the posse meant to save us from our unruly selves, our lawlessness. And you couldn't outrun and dodge them for long because they were old and out of shape and they might get tired and quit. You didn't want them to ever quit.

My aunt and my mother ran holding their sides. My mother may have been pregnant again. My father and uncle huffed along, red in the face, and I couldn't recall the last time I'd seen any of them run. I recollect that adults in the 1950s hurried, but they rarely ran. Only something deadly serious could make an adult run back then—some emergency, some vital contribution to a child's well-being. Up in the tree, I watched them chase Melissa, and I felt glad for her that she was so precious. She must have come to a similar conclusion when she trapped herself in the garage, must have sensed how they labored on her behalf, must have known she was lucky that four well-intentioned adults would go to such extremes. That she pouted long after receiving the shot, that she glared at my father for days after, whenever they crossed paths, I considered the ignorant demeanor of an ingrate. And although I never did so, I felt the impulse to roll up my sleeve in front of her, wave my little white muscle around like a flag of surrender, and offer myself to be shot.

Escape Artists

FALL, ARRIVING SLOWLY in North Carolina, began in late August when, despite the roaring heat, a single crimson dogwood leaf unhinged itself somewhere in a wood and dropped as quietly as blood. Deep in the shrubbery that ringed our porch, cicadas screamed a frantic, high-pitched, last-ditch effort at tunefulness. I detected fall in the bluer depth of shadows beneath trees and in the wanton way the maples showed the silver undersides of their leaves to the wind, like petticoats. There seemed a surly, murderous strength in the sunlight, despite shortening days. Yellow jackets chased me on the playground for a taste of the tart crisp apple my mother had packed in my lunch. Long before the leaves turned, the air felt both solemn and bright, as tremulous and festive as a drum roll. Something else was supposed to happen, not simply school, but something eagerly elsewhere.

After Labor Day we gave ourselves over to the routines of the school year: the stiff discipline of wearing shoes again, homework and piano lessons, the wholesome incentives supplied by scout troops. Then, one morning in October, just as we were all about to burst from

the plainness and stricture of our lives, our father made his wonderful
announcement.

"The fair's in town," he said. "Does anybody feel like going after
school?"

He spoke matter-of-factly, but it seemed that he was no longer but-
tering his breakfast toast. He polished it, and it gleamed in his hand
like a trophy while the cornflakes in our cereal bowls had turned into
nuggets of solid gold.

Just the word "fair"—a wand of a word—had transformed the beginning of an ordinary school day into one long uphill postponement
of pleasure, an Everest of hours. At school I watched the drowsy classroom clock suction to every minute. During "Show and Tell" I had
nothing to show but the battered sneakers by mother had suggested
I wear to the fairgrounds instead of slopping around in my good saddle oxfords. "After school," I told my classmates, affecting an air of
mystery, "I'm going to be ankle-deep in sawdust."

Alas, Tony Wadsworth guessed what I was up to and blurted the
secret right out. He was the boy every girl with any dignity—and we
all possessed huge harrumphs of dignity in fifth grade—avoided picking for a square dance partner because he had warts all over his hands.

Tony and his older brother had already visited the fair on opening
night, and to prove it he unrolled the cuffs of his jeans and deposited
a trickle of sawdust on the floor. The Wadsworth boys had been and
seen and conquered, Tony told the class with an air of superiority. And
they had not done any of the baby stuff either. No-siree. They'd ridden
the Bullet and the double-decker Ferris wheel and the Caterpillar.
They'd rammed a carload of teenage girls with their bumper car until
the girls cried.

The Caterpillar! My mother had never allowed me to ride the
Caterpillar—a tame amusement, really, except that the train of cars
looped the track at about sixty miles per hour and, at the ride's climax,

a hood of canvas unfurled and enshrouded you in darkness. It wasn't the speed of the ride that my mother considered dangerous; it was the germ-infested covering. "Do you want to catch polio?" she fussed. I took my seat, upstaged, while the whole class buzzed and babbled about the fair, making plans to outdo the bravado of their previous exploits. Out teacher, Mrs. Parker, let us blab straight through our scheduled math period. She was glad to see us impassioned for a change. She probably liked talking about the fair better than doing long division, too. She told us that we could talk about the fair as long as we liked—right through recess if that's what we wanted. *Recess.* It was the only word more powerfully seductive than *fair.*

After lunch, Mrs. Parker suggested that in lieu of our regular language arts assignments, we could write stories about our personal excursions to the fair. Or, she said, we could write about the circus. She wanted to appease certain malcontents whom she'd heard grumbling that the circus was more interesting. "In your papers," she said, "tell which you enjoy most and why. Take your time. Think before you write."

But for me it was no contest. Clearly the circus was a spectator sport while the fair was utterly participatory. Any kid knew, as he sat on a bleacher or gazed toward the spotlit ceiling of a circus tent, that the place he *aimed* on being was *up there,* toeing the high wire or dangling by his heels from the slippery bar of a trapeze.

So what if he fell? Falling was probably the best thing of all: whooshing down high luminous air-turned-sliding-board while the crowd gasped and screamed, hitting the safety net in the sweetest spot of its spring, and boomeranging skyward again while everybody cheered.

DANGER: that's what we went looking for as kids. Let the adults while away their time with caution. We kids were looking to be shaken loose, tumbled, stirred into dizzy blurs of ourselves, spooked, booby-trapped, lost. With its daredevil amusements and sinister ride operators, who wouldn't stop the Tilt-a-Whirl no matter how hard you begged, and parental admonitions about pickpockets and cheats, the fair loomed upon the bland horizon of our small southern town promising not merely bedazzlement but spine-tingling close calls. Perhaps even an invigorating brush with real wickedness.

I used to wonder why my father always announced his plan to take us to the fair at breakfast. Why didn't he simply drive up to the schoolyard that afternoon and surprise us with the jaunt? "The joy of anticipation," he'd told me once when I accused him of torture. He defended corralling us for church in much the same way. Not that we anticipated church—quite the opposite. Twitching in the pew, bopping one another on the head with paper fans stapled to Popsicle sticks, we anticipated *release* from its dark cave of holiness. "Be glad you're bored," he'd whisper to us as we whined and agonized. "The seed of imagination is boredom," my father said. And it's probably true that some of the most accomplished pictures I ever drew of horses and queens and monsters were completed in smeary pencil on the back of a church bulletin; and some ferocious daydreams that governed my muse for years grew out of unloosening the knots of childhood boredom that came of waiting.

I was a tangle of waiting through the last hour of school before the fair. I gazed out the window, casing the sky for changes in the weather, even prayed to God—who I was certain was a very Boring Person, someone who hadn't the slightest desire to scratch what itched and no doubt considered fairs trivial, dismissible ordeals—*please* don't let it rain a single drop. Not a minute before three o'clock did my father's Plymouth cruise up beside the flagpole.

As we set off for the Dixie Classic Fairgrounds, sweeping past school chums who waited for car pools or mounted their bicycles for rides home to dull routines of homework, it seemed that our car glided by like a parade float. We emanated a nimbus of privilege, riding tall in our seats like a royal family. Something about the way the sunlight jittered off the chrome of the dashboard, speckling the air, crowning the tops of our heads, seemed an anointment of bliss. When I spied my best girlfriend, waiting glumly for her mother to pick her up and take her to her piano lesson, I ducked below the window.

～❧

I believed I could hear and smell the fair—much like I could the ocean—long before I glimpsed it. I leaned out the car window to sniff and to cock an ear against the rush of glistening wind. I imagined the horizon seethed like a heat mirage and that in the distant sky I might catch sight of drifting balloons, toy-colored puffs like exotic smoke signals rising from the fairground's blaze of wonders.

We parked the Plymouth in a grassy field, directed by the gestures of volunteer attendants—local Jaycees and Shriners who also managed rival eateries inside the fair. Traditionally we ate a supper of homemade chili under the snappy red-and-white awning of the Shriners' tent.

My brothers and I danced jigs all the way across the parking field to the turnstile. By contrast, our parents seemed almost willfully slow: King and Queen of the Dawdlers, ambling behind us, my father leafing through his wallet and saying, "Oops, forgot to bring my money, kids. Sorry," trying to get our goat.

I was probably eleven that year; my oldest brother was nine. I'd been doing some baby-sitting in the neighborhood, proving that my accountability could extend beyond the family. I was, my parents often told me with prideful appraisal, growing up. But I would never have anticipated the breathtaking latitude that was accorded me at the admissions gate when my father handed me two five-dollar bills and granted me permission to grouse about the fair independently that year. On condition—here it came, there were *always* conditions—that I would oversee my oldest brother. Baby-sit him, so to speak. Keep him in sight, accompany him on all the rides.

I was wise to their ploy. The freedom offered was a ruse.

It was my brother Knothead whom they wanted to placate. *He* was

the one who'd been griping about all the baby rides they still expected
him to enjoy: the stupid little ponies trudging in a stupid little circle,
the stupid swishy-slow boats with their stupid clanging bells, the stupid miniature Ferris wheel with tot cages rather than open-air seats.
"Over my dead body," he'd howled when my parents had pointed to
the merry-go-round.

"All right then," my parents conceded. They'd take our youngest
brother, the true baby, to ride all the "stupid" stuff, and we could meet
them at six o'clock for supper in front of the Shriners' tent.

"How will we know when it's six?" I asked, feeling strangely uneasy when I ought to have been reeling with gratitude.

My mother gave my father a worried look. "Just ask somebody,"
she said. "But pick somebody who looks, well, *nice*."

I remember the woeful shrinking sensation of watching my parents disappear into the throng. I felt as small and as pocketable as a
Kewpie doll, and although he tried to shake me off, I fastened my
hand to my brother's.

We began with a few familiar rides first: the Scrambler and the
Swings. We took a stroll through the Laff-a-Minute Fun House. We
bought caramel-coated apples that clotted and wrenched our teeth,
and played a game where you tried to toss nickels onto plates. The
winner took home a plush pink teddy bear the size of a horse. I don't
know why teddy bears that large have such appeal. My mother would
have disparaged the thing as tacky. It would not have fit in our car.
But I was dead set on winning one and wasted a dollar's worth of
nickels in the effort.

Now that gambling had whet our appetites for seamier adventure,
we dipped into the long-forbidden freak show tent, where we wit-
nessed all manner of talent derived from human affliction and con-
ning: Alligator Lady, who had a complexion as ribbed and armored-
looking as a waffle; Torture Champ, who hammered nails up his
nostrils; two little girls, Siamese twins joined at the hip, who were
displayed in the family's living quarters—a kind of trailer-size aquarium—enjoying normal activities such as eating popcorn and watching *Lassie* on TV.

"It's all fake," Knothead informed me when we vacated the tent. "Alligator Lady wears some kind of creepy makeup. Torture Champ uses rubber nails. The twins are glued together with school paste. The joke's on us. Can we ride the roller-coaster now?"

But I felt subdued by the freak show. I wished suddenly that my mother or my father were standing close by to corroborate Knothead's judgment, to tell me that the freaks were not tragic but making a good livelihood out of fooling the public. I'd hit a puzzling spot of drabness in the fair's high-gloss shine. I'd glimpsed things plaintively human beyond the surface hype of the freaks: goosebumps on Alligator Lady's arms when she removed her sweater to display her skin, Torture Champ's wedding ring—it looked just like my father's— which kept snagging on the nails he planted in his nose. The Siamese twins were about my own age. Their dresses were soiled and they both needed to blow their noses. They bickered over which television channel to watch until their mother, wearing a floppy housedress and kitchen-drudge head rag, clunked peevishly onstage to settle their hash. I thought that any second she was going to settle mine, too. "Just what are *you* gawking at?" I expected her to say. My own mother would have asked me that. My own mother would have nudged me back onto the midway, would have told me that it was rude to stare.

I wasn't supposed to be missing my parents at the fair, but after the freak show I did. A need for consolation persisted. Even as I hung upside-down in the Bullet. Even as the Caterpillar's cocoon of doom rolled over our heads or we plummeted into the deepest shrieking valley of the Killer-Coaster. We threw up our hands; we screamed bloody murder, begged for mercy, every follicle of our hair ramrodded with fear. But at the end of each ride, there was just the two of us, quaking. No parent waved cheerily as we twirled around the bend. Nobody stood below us on the ground, looking frightened for our sakes. There was no one who genuinely cared whether or not we fell and dashed our brains out. Nobody to gainsay our bravery, but nobody to applaud it either.

After one last death-defying ride on the Round-Up, I stood beside my brother amid the gaudy whir of the midway, wiping tears from my cheeks. They were, I think, the jubilant tears of survival, of relief that the ride was over, of both excitement and terror for my depart-ing childhood.

Although the dangerous adult rides were twice the price of chil-dren's, I still had more than a dollar left. But I pressed the money far into the recesses of my pockets until my pockets felt empty. Twilight thickened the air. A sweet homey smell like pickle relish and creamed coffee and warm red chili quickened my breathing. I was thinking about the familiar splintery rasp of the Shriners' wooden benches and the way my father liked to loop an arm around my mother's waist while he ate, and of how my youngest brother would probably already be nodding off to sleep in my mother's lap. I recalled that many of the Shriners were loyal patients of my father's and that he enjoyed swap-ping stories with them. The sound of fatherly men laughing together was as happy a sound as I knew. There might even be one of the Shriners' Band members eating supper at a nearby table, decked out in his sultan's gear replete with fez and saber. We would want to exam-ine the saber, run our fingertips bravely along the blade to test its sharpness. Only we would have to ask our parents' permission first.

After supper we drove home, sitting shoulder-to-shoulder in the dark, the lights of the fairground guttering behind us. In the distance, it all seemed very beautiful, but I didn't have to turn around to know this.

At a stoplight, my mother leaned forward to turn down Perry Como on the radio. "Did you and Knothead have fun?" she asked me.

"Oh yes," I said quickly.

"What was the best thing of all?" she asked.

"The Caterpillar," Knothead told her without remorse.

Sitting in the backseat of the Plymouth, I felt warm and sleepy and spent. My baby brother was sprawled in my lap. My baby brother who'd done all the baby stuff at the fair. His eyes were shut, his mouth ringed clownishly with the cherry stain of a Sno-cone. He held a pinwheel, like a flower, against his chest. His shoes had eaten up his socks. *"This* was the best thing," I said to my mother, touching the dreaming child, watching her eyes follow and approve the sweep of my fingers through my sleeping brother's hair. "This," I said, meaning, now, the ongoing spectacle of who we were *now.* Not the fair's seductive glory, not the turbulent rides nor death defied nor life lived to the hilt. But "This," meaning our ordinary selves, life before and after that framed and contained enchantment: that explosive hurly-burly from which we had emerged intact. We were like transcendent survivors of a glamorous stunt, escape artists unbound, vanishing acts returned to plain sweet Earth and heading home.

TRUTHS AND GRIT

I Was Impeached

UNTIL I WAS elected president of Mrs. Parker's fifth grade class, the closest I'd come to politics was the patriotic thrill of standing alongside my Grandmother Ruth on Elm Street, downtown, handing out paper poppies on Veterans Day for the American Legion Auxiliary. On her lapel, my grandmother wore a tiny, brightly enameled American flag. She stood staunch as granite, tight-lipped with mission. She and my grandfather were straight-ticket Democrats. My father had voted for Ike. Since the discussion of politics was taboo when our family gathered for Sunday dinner, my child's impression was that politics was an unsavory institution that imperiled harmony.

Being class president was like being elected to the position of hood ornament: you served as an official adornment, walking tall and serene, a model of good behavior. You lead your class to assemblies, to the playground and the cafeteria. You represented them at weekly student council meetings. Those meetings, held in the school library, may have gotten you out of arithmetic, but they were supervised by our strict commandant of a librarian, Mrs. Shelburn, whose eyeglasses bulged the size and scope of binoculars. We were a parliament flawed by yawning and wriggle-itis, loathsome offenses so magnified under Mrs. Shelburn's scrutiny that repeat offenders were frequently banished from the assembly and sent skulking back to their classrooms. The meetings schooled us in a pious, sober-minded civility, much like church, and trained us to be rule-mongers. We debated and voted on rules for safer playground activity, rules for fire drills and cafeteria clean-up, rules pertaining to washroom and library courtesy.

The meetings were so constrictive that I yearned to resign, but I admired the standards of forbearance and compliance with which my predecessor had borne his responsibilities and I sought to copy him. Jim Van Hecke, who'd stepped down from office after a semester's service, had acquired a presidential manner during his term. He strode the corridors of Sternberger Elementary School with lanky confidence. He didn't blow up his empty Popsicle bags and explode them at lunch like the other boys did. The presidency had matured him. He looked taller, perhaps even a little gray at the temples, a junior, beardless version of Abe Lincoln, and every girl had a crush on him. When we studied the Bill of Rights, he knew them in order. While he explained "parliamentary procedure," the girls on the front row swooned.

Unlike Jim Van Hecke, I had no natural talent for understanding the mechanics of government. My friends had gotten me elected because they liked *me,* not my vacant platform, and after my ascent to office, I basked in the belief that popularity could substitute for integrity and vision. Truthfully, I became a little cocky with privilege. It's a heady thing to always get to be first in line.

One fateful day, not long after my election, Mrs. Parker abruptly announced that she needed to leave the room. We wondered if she was in the throes of a nicotine fit. We all knew she smoked Pall Malls. She'd ruefully admitted her craving to us the day we'd studied the respiratory system. She'd opened her voluminous purse, extracted a cigarette, lit it in class, taken a few puffs, then rummaged in her desk

for a Kleenex. After inhaling deeply, she'd held the tissue to her lips
and blown smoke through it. When she peeled the tissue away from
her mouth, we could see where her breath had soiled it a pale muddy
color. Appropriately horrified, we'd admonished her to quit smoking.
She'd promised that she would try; but she was no good at it. She was
an *addict,* she'd told us, shaking her head with probably the same degree of public remorse I'd felt when I'd opened my last report card in
front of my friends and out had slammed the first C of my life. It had
seemed to swizzle my scrawny neck like a horseshoe, then thump
heavily upon my chest like a collar, yoking me to ineptitude.

As Mrs. Parker hastened out the door, she paused at the threshold
to flick off the overhead lights. "Everybody, put your heads down on
your desks and take a little rest. Absolutely no talking. Not a peep,"
she cautioned. "Marianne, please be our room monitor. Take down
the names of anybody who so much as whispers."

From my binder I detached a crisp new sheet of Blue Horse note-
book paper, big-lined. My pencils were all sharp. I did not have to put
my head on my desk like all the other sheep. I was in charge: the *presidential* monitor. I wrote down Todd McKay's name because he was
talking nonstop to Jim Van Hecke. I did not see Jim's lips moving
back. Jim had his head on his desk, just like Mrs. Parker had requested. Once Todd McKay had beaned me with a baseball bat—it
was the only way he knew how to flirt. Well, *Wham-o* to you, Todd
McKay, I said to myself and underlined his name because he hadn't
shut up since the lights went off.

I took down Bob Zane's name because he was messing with Barbara Nelson's pony-tail. I didn't count it against her that she kept
wheeling around in her seat to defend herself. I took down Linwood
Collins's name because he was hurling spitwads at the ceiling. I wrote
down Mark Silvers's name, even though he'd been my boyfriend in
fourth grade. He was trying to rouse everybody to sing "Happy Birthday" even though it wasn't anyone's birthday. He dashed up to the
chalkboard and put erasers on top of his head to make people laugh.
Pam Atkinson and Carolyn Dees laughed, but I didn't count it against
them because, if I hadn't been monitor, I would have laughed, too.

Charles Snipes kept cracking his knuckles and burping on purpose. He could burp an entire stanza of "The Star Spangled Banner" on one long gravelly monotone of effluvia. "Shhh!" Jim Van Hecke warned his pals. Should I have written his name down for *so much as whispering?* I excused him on account of his being the ex-president.

By the time Mrs. Parker returned, I'd written down eight names out of a classroom of thirty children. All the names belonged to boys. Mrs. Parker delivered a stern speech about responsibility and growing up and rudeness and respect. As she read the list, each boy shrunk from the sound of his name as if it were the crack of a whip. Then she made each boy copy an entire page, comma for comma, word for microscopic word, out of her big red Merriam-Webster dictionary. To copy a single page from that dictionary *neatly* took hours: hours that removed a student from recess and lunch in the cafeteria. It was a brutal and lonesome punishment, an intellectual Siberia. But the command to write with methodical care is what took a toll on the boys.

I'm not sure when I first heard the word "impeach." Mrs. Parker might have defined it when we studied the executive, legislative, and judicial branches of the government. It had struck me as an odd word, but its definition made sense. First, you were regarded as a perfect peach; then you did something wrong and your accusers reassessed your peachiness.

Before studying the Constitution, I'd thought there was no way to get rid of a president in office unless he died or was assassinated. The knowledge that he could be impeached and tried for a number of public trust breaches made the president seem human to me, not above reproach, capable of humility and remorse. I wondered if, as a new president, you might start out peachily but, over time and due to the demands of the office, find that your peachiness had wizened. I thought of peaches as baby-faced fresh. Harry Truman looked tart as a lemon. Ike looked bland as an egg. Would-be president Adelaide Stevenson stood as lean and unfrilly as rhubarb. Vice-president Nixon's nose sat curvaceously on his face like a sweet gherkin pickle. Somewhere out there, although I had no knowledge of this at the time, John Kennedy was grooming his peachiness, and peachiness would figure prominently in what got him elected.

"Impeach" was a delicious new word to us; it made our brains salivate. New vocabulary turned us into mouthy hybrids of innocence and sophistication. It was like being handed a potent new tool that would help us pry loose the secretive lids that held us apart from the grown-up world. The boys in Mrs. Parker's fifth grade did not take long to mobilize. The day after their punishments, emboldened by their knowledge of the mechanics of democracy, miffed at the injustices their gender had suffered in the slave labor camp of the Merriam-Webster dictionary, they began to grumble among themselves. The word "impeach" jabbed its way out of their huddle like a chiseling, pointed finger. On the playground they segregated themselves from us girls, talked low, guffawed, cast devious, spurning looks in my direction. A paper and pencil passed among them.

Although he did not sign the petition requesting my impeachment, I'm certain it was Jim Van Hecke's knowledge of protocol that the boys solicited and followed. After recess and washroom break, eight plaintiffs appeared before the High Counsel of Mrs. Parker in an orderly, rational assembly to vent their grievances. Their brows rumpled with expressions of earnest suffering, not anger. They'd scrubbed up in the washroom, tucked in their shirts, and all of them smelled like green goo soap. They bore no resemblance to the scoundrels and hoodlums we knew them to be. They conducted themselves with the distressed dignity of a wronged people.

"We officially impeach her," they told Mrs. Parker, unfurling the petition on her desk. "Now we want to elect a new president. One that doesn't hate all the boys in our class."

"Marianne doesn't hate all the boys," Jim Van Hecke gently amended. "Do you?" He looked me kindly in the eye. He would go on in life to run for public office and lose because, like Jimmy Carter, he was more empathetic than shrewd.

Mrs. Parker listened to every word against me that the malcontents spoke. She provided them due process. She nodded gravely a time or two, conveying both understanding and sympathy. Then she corrected our understanding of "impeachment." The word didn't necessarily mean one's removal from office, she said. It only meant accusation and then, perhaps, a trial. It didn't necessarily mean that you were no longer a peach, if you were impeached, she said. It meant that a few— and not necessarily the majority—had questioned your peachiness, that your peachiness was in doubt, but not disproved. Who knew but what a rotten apple—or two or three or *eight*—might be stirring up trouble for a peach.

It was Friday afternoon, almost time for the dismissal bell. "If the class feels like it, we can all stay after school for further discussion," Mrs. Parker suggested. "Although impeachment preliminaries might drag into the night."

It was unanimous that we adjourn until Monday.

I didn't seek my parents' advice or consolation over the weekend. I think I was too ashamed. I was a child who valued pleasing the people I loved over almost anything. My girlfriends were uncharacteristically silent about the matter. Perhaps they were embarrassed for me. Perhaps they felt that my discredit compromised their judgment in having chosen me for a friend. At an age when boys were beginning to brandish romantic torches for some of us, I suspected that a few of my friends, favoring secret crushes, verged on switching loyalties.

I felt marooned. Those swift glib moments of writing down the names of boys who most annoyed me, who were, I'd thought, dispensable to my happiness, had sentenced me to a sort of solitary confinement so extreme that I would have welcomed even the Merriam-Webster's tedious company.

On Monday morning, Mrs. Parker marched to the front of the room and stood with her hand over her heart while we faced the flag to recite the Pledge of Allegiance. She looked luminous with good news—we thought maybe she'd quit smoking—and after we'd seated ourselves, she proposed the bold amendments to our classroom Constitution that ultimately exonerated me.

There would be no more single room monitors, she decreed. The job placed too heavy a burden on the monitor to tattletale. In the future, she would appoint two monitors: a boy to take down the names of boys who misbehaved and a girl to have the same jurisdiction over the girls. There would be no more copying out of the Merriam-Webster either, she said. It was a miserable punishment, nonrehabilitative, mind-pinching busywork. From that day forward she would think up more creative punishments that better suited the crime. "For instance," she said to Bob Zane, "if you persist in trying to catch flies while we do arithmetic, you will be sent out in the hall to sit in a chair with a bottle until you have caught ten flies alive." Everybody laughed.

"This is the way our government is *supposed* to work," she told us. "Complaints are brought forth; leaders listen attentively and consider alternatives. Laws are amended or abolished if they don't serve justice as the people regard that it ought to be served. 'By, for, and of the People,' that's what the Constitution guarantees our government will be," she said. "You *are* the People." It gave me goose bumps.

During the Clinton-Lewinsky scandal, when I saw the newspaper headline PRESIDENT IMPEACHED, I felt a tumultuous empathy. It was the worst of childhood that I suddenly recalled: humiliation that sprang from poor judgment, the shallow craving to be popular, arbitrary biases against the opposite sex, the ignorant assumption that my election to office made me unassailable. I'm here to testify that the stigma of impeachment does not detach any more than one's guilty fingerprints or one's less than peachy reflection staring back from a mirror. Even though my presidency was rescued by Mrs. Parker's insights and correctives, my remorse persisted, and I ruled timidly thereafter, the lamest of ducks.

Since I still live in the town where I grew up and he often visits relatives here, I've occasionally run into Jim Van Hecke. Although we cheerfully converse, I can't help wondering to this day if the first thing he thinks of when he sees me is my impeachment. It's not paranoia as much as the long shadow of accountability that certain trials of childhood cast. I wonder what sort of politico Bill Clinton was in elementary school. Maybe he was swift at politics but chased the girls on the playground until he made somebody cry. Would it have changed the outcome of history if Bill Clinton had been impeached as a boy? As for me, I slunk away from politics for good.

In my judgmental role as room monitor, taking down the boys' names my pencil had seemed to smoke. I'd activated the Mrs. Shelburn in myself. Of course I couldn't have sustained her rigid pose, not me, a kid whose shoelaces were always unraveling to trip her up, whose undone sashes trailed in the wind, who usually had a button missing, who tended to procrastinate her homework and who liked to clown around as much as anyone. But briefly I'd succeeded at being somebody fiercely *other,* a ramrod of certitude, a stickler. Mine was the sort of experiment in identity that gets a kid into trouble now and again, but helps us eventually to sort out who we are—if our bluff gets called enough.

White Girl's Burden

TOM DOODLEY WAS the black tenant farmer who lived on my grandfather's land when my father was growing up in Pleasant Garden, a swath of rolling countryside south of Greensboro, North Carolina. The man's actual last name wasn't Doodley, but when he called the chickens to come get their feed, he cried, "Doodley, doodley, doodley," in a high-pitched, singsong voice. My father, who was a young boy at the time, nicknamed the man Tom Doodley and Tom liked the name, so it stuck.

Tom and his wife, Martha, lived in a cabin behind my grandparents' farmhouse. My grandfather, a doctor, worked in Greensboro at the county courthouse, where he served a long tenure as one of Guilford County's first public health officers. He was a gentleman farmer, and although his acreage was small, he hired Tom to maintain the property and help with chores. Tom grew a garden, milked one cow, and raised chickens. He and Martha sold eggs. He helped my father build a little hatchery and raise chicks, and on the agonizing winter night when the hatchery caught fire and hundreds of chicks burned up, he held my sobbing father back from the flames, trying his best to comfort him.

The entire community was fond of Tom. He was smart, patient, industrious, a ready hand. My father idolized Tom and hung on him like a shadow.

One moonlit summer night, Tom and Martha set off to attend services at a nearby country church. They didn't own a car and so they walked. It was a pleasant and bright night out. After church, they started home along the same dusty road where, not far from my grandfather's farmstead, a car loaded with drunk white men bore down on them. As Martha later reported, it appeared that the men merely wanted to frighten her and Tom, to scatter them off the road and into the ditch. But after they had done so and driven past, the men turned the car around and sought them out again. When they discovered Tom scrambling to leap out of the way, they plowed into him, then drove off fast.

My father was around ten years old at the time and vividly remembered Martha hollering on the front porch for my grandfather. He remembered standing at his bedroom window, praying that Tom was still alive, watching as his father and Martha rode off into the black bright night to look for Tom's body and confirm what Martha already believed was true: that Tom had been killed by a hit-and-run driver.

The men were eventually apprehended, their identification expedited by an observant garage mechanic hired to repair a dented fender flecked with blood. My grandfather—who had courthouse connections—pushed for the law's fullest vengeance upon the men, but finally they were given light sentences, stemming from manslaughter convictions, not cold-blooded murder.

Had the men intended to kill Tom, or did the tragic episode result from a drunken joyride gone awry? It was 1930, on a back road near a small town in North Carolina. Nighttime. No witnesses. If the men had intended to kill Tom, was it because he was black or because they thought they could get away with such a crime—or a combination of both? Here came Tom and Martha, shuffling down a dark road, vulnerable in their anonymity and possibly objects of racist scorn. They were easy prey.

In telling the story of Tom's death, my father never directly accused the men of killing Tom because he was black, but he *implied* it, as I'm sure his own father must have done. I heard implication in the apologetic tone of his voice, the heavy look of burden in his face. Whenever he told the story, it was clear that he still missed Tom, that he believed Tom's life had been purposely wasted by three miscreants he was loath to call southerners.

My father loved the South, and he loved North Carolina in particular, with a maudlin and fierce patriotism. He could not bear anything to be wrong with his country. It was clear to him that Tom had been a victim of something that living a discreet, humane, and productive life could not protect him from. But that something sprung from the ill will of three misfits, not any widespread cultural malice.

In telling the story, he sometimes softened its brutality by including an anecdote about the men from the black funeral parlor who, upon hearing of Tom's death, alighted like scavenger crows on Martha's doorstep the next morning, offering to trade her the down payment on a fancy casket for the lot of her chickens. My vigilant grandmother, overhearing the commotion, peered out her back door to see two black men in mourning coats and top hats scurrying around the barnyard, trying to snatch chickens and stuff them into feed sacks. She promptly ordered the men off the property, and my grandfather paid for Tom's funeral.

I think my father meant his anecdote to suggest that if Tom had been killed by one kind of white person, Tom's wife had been rescued by another. It wasn't that my grandmother's pragmatic virtue countered the crime done to Tom, but noting her feisty defense of Martha's chickens seemed to score a reassuring point for accountability and goodness, at the very least.

My father believed that goodness would prevail against the most corrupting odds. He trusted and admired his parents, loved God and country, was grateful to have been born into the circumstances of his upbringing. I remember his parents as laconic Victorians. My grandfather, a man respected for his integrity and humanitarian skills, impressed me as a morose, slow-moving man with a stony Mount

Rushmore face. Rarely detached from his armchair, he seemed as impassive as the furniture itself. In the summertime, when the lawn needed cutting, it was my grandmother who put on shorts and marched through the weeds with a push mower.

But my father had known them in their heyday of championing the underdog Tom Doodley. Of all the hundreds of stories he told me about his boyhood, the story in which their haloes gleamed most radiantly was the story about Tom. It was probably the most influential story my father ever told me and may have set me on my writer's course. Now I will begin to tell you why I think so.

In 1957 a student in my fifth grade class—I will call her Mary Smith —accompanied her parents to a PTA meeting at Sternberger Elementary School. Mary Smith was new in town; her parents had recently moved to Greensboro from a large midwestern city. Her father, retired from playing professional sports, was something of a celebrity, and our school community was proud to welcome them. Mr. Helberg, our principal, was perhaps a little starstruck himself.

At some point during the PTA meeting, Mary Smith began to twitch with boredom. Or she announced that she was thirsty or claimed she needed to use the restroom. Her parents gave her permission to leave the school auditorium and monitor herself. This was 1957 in an all-white, affluent section of a small southern town where most kids I knew rode their bicycles to school and parents never gave a thought to their well-being or safety. There simply was no crime. Our section of town was called Starmount Forest and the city police department assigned one officer, Sergeant Craddock, to patrol our streets. Everybody knew Sergeant Craddock, a plump, grandfatherly, and soft-spoken man who served as school crossing guard in the mornings outside Sternberger Elementary. His wife sometimes babysat for us. As a hobby, the Craddocks raised albino parakeets, and we children visited them and were always welcomed. That our patrolman raised parakeets and invited us into his house to see them should say everything about the neighborhood in which I grew up.

Mary Smith and I were never more than marginal friends. I remember her as small, wiry, and athletic, about my size. She had wavy, chocolate brown shoulder-length hair and a flat brown velvety mole on one cheek. She was a powerful kickball player.

We liked Mary and included her, we popular and established girls, but I don't recall feeling intimate with her, whispery and secretive. She was too high strung and mouthy for whispering. She was bossy, and I was bossy, too, so we learned to tolerate one another without conceding much ground. I retain the dim impression that Mary Smith was disloyal to me in some way, that once she reneged on a invitation. She'd promised to invite me somewhere and ended up inviting someone else. This may be a trick of my vengeful memory. Probably what I remember about the girl is shaded by what actually did happen.

During the PTA meeting, Mary Smith left her parents' jurisdiction and wandered down a corridor. Perhaps she used the bathroom or sipped water from the fountain. But after she had done what she'd requested to do, she did not return to the auditorium. Instead she went exploring. Snooping might be a more accurate word.

Coy, the school custodian, was making his evening rounds with the push broom when he heard Mary Smith rattling about. She'd slipped into an unlocked classroom—it may have been our fifth grade room—and had found some way of entertaining herself in the dark. It must have been spooky and thrilling for her to find herself alone in the room, twirling around, opening drawers, maybe strumming the autoharp, perching on the teacher's stool and pretending authority, leafing through the heavy volume of *Jack Tales* that Mrs. Parker kept on her desk. There was nobody to tell her to keep her mitts to herself, to quiet down, to take her seat, to wait her turn. Later, when I heard the story, I imagined myself playing around in the dark classroom just like Mary. It might have been something she'd dared herself to do. I might have done the same, given the opportunity.

There were two versions about what happened next.

Coy's version was that he'd heard suspicious sounds in the classroom and turned on a light to investigate, surprising and perhaps frightening Mary, who thought herself to be completely alone in that part of the building. He chastened her for being where she was not supposed to be and dismissed her—perhaps gruffly. If he had touched her—and he could not remember doing so—it was to guide her out of the room, like tugging the halter of a reluctant mule, because at first she resisted his order that she leave and insisted she had permission to be there. Coy vowed that he had spoken to Mary as someone authorized to protect her. She had been found off limits. As custodian, he was carrying out his duty to safeguard the school against intruders.

Mary's version, supported by her parents, was that Coy had discovered her whereabouts and had reprimanded her for trespassing. When she protested, Coy threatened her with punishment and then cornered her and forced her to kiss him on the mouth before letting her go.

Perhaps, Coy suggested, he'd overwhelmed Mary Smith with his insistence that she was in the wrong. Perhaps she'd accused him of kissing her because she'd felt angered by his admonishment, felt caught in some unlawful act, made to feel ashamed, dressed down by a janitor. She'd felt entitled to get even.

Coy's word was respected. He had worked as custodian at Sternberger Elementary since the school had opened in 1949. I remember him as a pleasant middle-aged man, tall, lanky, quiet, dutiful. His female counterpart was a woman named Callie—we children thought they were sweethearts, but they weren't. Coy and Callie sat outside their broom closet in gray folding chairs, eating their sandwiches for lunch. They wore gray uniforms. They smiled and waved back to us as we filed down the corridors, on our way to the library or the cafeteria. They liked being spoken to. They beamed and grinned, and I would bet that now and again they even felt appreciated. They were distinct from the indifferent women in head rags who dished up soup in the cafeteria. They mingled, could be depended upon to rescue us from our endless messes, unflinchingly mopping up puddles of vomit or spilled milk with a single swift swab of the mop. They bore trays of cafeteria food through the rain to a class of children who met in the scout hut behind the school. They stoked coal into the furnace to keep us warm, waxed acres of linoleum floors. There was no graffiti at Sternberger School because of Callie and Coy. The bathrooms sparkled. There was never a shortage of toilet paper or brown paper

towels or green goo soap. The whole school smelled of their deter-
gents and dusting rags, the husky dry sweep of their brooms pushing
rubbery crumbs of dirt-erasing powder scented with wintergreen,
smells as amiable as the velvety dog-eared aroma of the card catalogue,
the caramel smell of lacquer on new tables and desks, the furry, cedary
fragrance of pencil-sharpener shavings, the metallic scent of handlebars and jungle gyms stamped into everybody's flesh.

> Hail Sternberger, the best school in the land!
> We have an orchestra, and we have a band,
> We have singing; hear it ringing?
> Three cheers for our great school!
>
> Hail Sternberger, our teachers never rest,
> Three R's they teach us and insist we do our best.
> They work harder to make us smarter,
> Three cheers for our great school!
>
> Hail Sternberger, your colors green and white,
> Shining so brightly every day and every night.
> Forward leaning, truth we're gleaning,
> Three cheers for our great school!

Coy had never been in any sort of trouble before. His loyal record
of subordination, his agreeable and accommodating manner ought to
have exonerated him, but he had been accused of an unspeakable act.
Child molestation was not much in the news in those days and, because of the rare exposure, seemed even more heinous and undeniable a crime than today, when regressive-memory gurus and talk show
hosts coax reports of victimization out of nearly everybody.

Word of Mary Smith's accusation stunned and alarmed my own
parents, but they were not about to jump on any bandwagon without
being convinced by the facts. The facts, however, were sketchy and
concluded separate realities. Mary Smith said that Coy had kissed her.
Coy sorrowfully protested that he had not. Who you believed depended upon what you feared most: untruth or injustice.

I thought Mary Smith was a liar. I had never felt deeply companionable with her, and I distrusted her the way children learn to

distrust other children they can't depend on. Children are literalists. They appreciate honest declaration over hedgy innuendo. They trust action over postponement. They expect friends to represent their true selves to one another, not picturesque or metaphorical versions.

I'd been forthright in my overtures of friendship toward Mary Smith, and yet she'd lurked on the edge of my offerings with the sly demeanor of a fair-weather friend. We weren't pals because she couldn't commit to my high-risk standards of friendship. Something better might come along for her. I didn't like girls who held themselves in reserve like that. I liked girls who crawled side-by-side with me out onto the wobbliest branch.

But apart from my judgment of Mary's duplicity, I knew firsthand the vindictive cruelty lodged secretly in the hearts of young girls. I knew from experience that it was possible to convey yourself like a little princess, be teacher's pet, love Jesus so much that you wanted to marry him and, that failing, want to marry your preacher because you had a crush on goodness, on being good, pretty is as pretty does, your heart marching toward goodness all the time, your feet in patent leather Mary Janes and scalloped ankle socks, a little purse swinging on your arm and filled with half your week's allowance for the church collection plate. It was possible to clearly know right from wrong, to be pure in word and thought and deed, to champion the underdog, save bugs from spider webs, not stomp ants, play a baby game like Candyland with the child who lived across the street because it would make your mother proud. It was possible to be a shining example, a sunbeam for Jesus, the darling of the neighborhood and then, for some astonishing reason—perhaps jealousy, greed, or the thrill of domination—turn, as if bewitched, into a mean and furious demonling of destruction, besmirching your goodly self, sprouting wilfulness and treachery like fangs, talons, a rat's bristling tail.

This had happened to me more than once, but the most memorable of my transformations had occurred in first grade while standing in line to march to the cafeteria for lunch. I wanted to be cow's tail. I wanted to be last in line, a position of privilege in those days. Anita Jones, a sallow, round-faced girl with doleful, cornflower blue eyes wanted to be last in line, too. Everybody felt sorry for Anita because her mother had died when she was a baby. Her father had remarried—it wasn't that she was an orphan or had only an inept and bumbling father to care for her. But she was the only child in our class who was not being raised by her real mother, and she was stigmatized. I was impressed that Anita got through her days as well as she did. I could not imagine life without my mother, and so I pitied Anita. There was something about her tangled hair, the way her shoes always ate up her socks, that made her seem haphazard and forlorn. Normally I was respectful, even deferential around her. There was something about standing too close to her that always made me feel melancholy.

But on this particular day, both of us claiming the revered position of cow's tail with pouty, glaring insistence, I dismissed all sympathetic impulse. We were competitors, fair and square. We shoved one another in and out of the line—*where was our teacher?* We shouted that we hated one another. Some savage sense of my advantage heated my argument with her past my control. I was spewing rage. I seized upon her greatest weakness and throttled her with it. I laughed in her face, one of those merciless, spitty nonlaughs that bullies are known for, and I shouted at Anita Jones that I was glad her mother was dead.

Of course she dissolved into tears and wouldn't be consoled, even when the teacher flushed me out as her tormenter and I apologized. I was in agony. I did not want to be cow's tail ever again. My remorse over my hateful behavior could not have felt more palpable had I been tarred and feathered. I knew on the spot that I would never forget my miscarriage of power, that my cruelty toward Anita Jones would haunt me for life—and it has. The urge to triumph over someone weaker than oneself when one feels compromised by that person has generated much injustice in the world. That urge within me inflicted itself on Anita and perhaps it had overpowered Mary Smith's logic when she felt belittled by Coy's admonishment. She was the princess, after all, and he was the troll.

Maybe Mary Smith felt entitled to her lie because she knew that she could get away with it. That the lie saved her from embarrassment meant less to her than the power she wielded merely by being believed. Who would believe a troll's story above a princess's? By the same token, what little girl whose family adored her and gave her the moon could fail to have a generous heart? What little girl who had been treated so fairly in life could whimsically heap so dire a lie upon an innocent man? What sort of privileged child could break a person's heart to their face? I knew what sort of child because I had been one.

It was 1957 and a young white girl had pointed an accusing finger at a middle-aged black man. The police were never summoned, the media never informed. Coy sought no legal representation. Instead the matter was investigated by Greensboro Public School officials, and Coy agreed with them—although forswearing his guilt—that *under the circumstances* he should resign from his job.

Coy promptly left Sternberger School and found local factory work at Pomona Clay Products. The janitor who replaced him, a darker, more disgruntled-looking man, was named Lonnie. His standoffishness may have been a requirement for his employment.

Under the circumstances. I can only contemplate Coy's circumstances as having been the complete reversal of my own. Both of us were living in Greensboro, North Carolina, in the mid-fifties. It would be several more years before the first sit-in at the lunch counter of the now famous Woolworth's on Elm Street, February 1, 1960. Although there were poor white people in our community—mostly the mill workers—the only poor people I saw up close were black, and I didn't know any rich ones.

Sometimes my girlfriend Pam and I rode with Pam's mother to deliver to poor people clothing collected by the Junior League. We never went to the homes of white people. We drove down muddy, potholed lanes to grim little cinder-block houses or shacks that looked patched together out of cardboard and corrugated sheet metal. The sky above the houses was yellow because of the smoke from a nearby fertilizer plant.

It seemed that we always delivered the clothing on freezing cold days and that the children, who scattered as we drove up, were outside playing without coats on and barefooted. They ran up to the car and helped unload the boxes. They smelled mulchy. Their noses were crusty with snot and they had hard dry feet and brittle laughter. Pam and I tended to glamorize their lives. Despite their bitter plots and circumstances, their pluck made them seem heroic. It was fabulous to watch them dauntlessly running around without shoes or coats while snow flurries spangled the air and no mother shouted for them to do otherwise.

Pam and I lived in a tidy suburban neighborhood and our mothers had maids. Etta Williams was the poorest maid my mother ever hired; she sometimes worked extra hours baby-sitting us at night, but she would fall asleep before we were in bed because she was so old and exhausted. Mother constantly gave her packages of clothing and food. Once, after the pair of dyed chicks we'd gotten for Easter started growing up and were not so easily contained in their box, my mother gave them to Etta, who took them home, fattened them up on table scraps and eventually ate them. Our dog Lady ran after a maid who didn't work for us and bit her, unprovoked, on the ankle. My father made us get rid of the dog, and I felt sorry for the frightened maid, but Lady had never bitten anyone before. The fact that the woman was black impressed itself upon my child's mind and caused me to equate blacks not only with poverty but victimhood as well.

The county courthouse, downtown near the soon-to-be-famous Woolworth's, was the first building I ever saw that had separate drinking fountains for blacks and whites. COLORED ONLY, read a sign above one fountain. There was a separate prison unit for Negroes as well, where, once, when my grandfather took me along with him on his rounds, I saw a black inmate washing her clothes in a toilet and hanging them up to dry in her cell.

In the part of the world where I was growing up, black people were uniformly poor, they drank colored water, they sometimes had to wash their clothes in the toilet, they cleaned up other people's messes, ate the thrown-away pets of white children, got bitten by dogs.

Downtown, at the Carolina movie theater, black people had a separate ticket booth and side entrance. They were required to sit in the balcony. From my child's perspective, black people had only one true privilege over whites: they got to sit in the back of the bus. Once I'd tried to do it, but the bus driver had told me snappishly that it wasn't allowed. The rule was that black people got to be the cow's tail, *always* and without intervention.

Coy left his employment at Sternberger Elementary in 1957, eight years after he'd been hired. "He left voluntarily," Mr. Helberg, my former principal now retired, told me recently by phone. "Fortunately, there wasn't a scandal. Mary's parents couldn't have been nicer. They didn't want to press charges and so the situation was investigated by our own school people. Today," Mr. Helberg admitted, "it would have been a different story, but the media never got hold of this."

"What about the issue of race?" I asked him.

"Race was never an issue," he said.

Not long after Coy went to work for the Pomona factory, he was killed in a plant accident. I remember a stunned silence falling across our breakfast table as my father read the news article. The paper reported that Coy had been electrocuted.

It's possible that he was the first man I ever knew who died. I can't think of anyone who might have preceded him, for I was still young and innocent of death and it would be another year or so before my grandfather died and I glimpsed my father crying for the first time in my life.

Mary Smith had not returned to Sternberger for sixth grade. The family seemed to fade away from our community after Mary's accusation—or this is how I remember it. First she was there—center stage, pointing her finger, causing a man to lose his job—and then she disappeared. The man disappeared and the girl who had caused his disappearance disappeared as well.

I don't remember that she announced her family's plan for departure. There were no rumors of her father being transferred. I do recall tooling around on my bicycle and riding past her empty house one afternoon and thinking that her house had always looked empty, even when she'd lived in it. There had always been weeds in the yard and paint chipping off the bricks—an untended and slapdash look about the place that extended to my feelings about Mary herself. She had swooped hastily into our lives, set off sparks, heedlessly, for the worse, then run off, not having to watch while the fire she'd set burned every-thing down. Nobody knew where the Smiths had gone. Nobody talked about them anymore. They'd blown in, done their damage, then blown out again, as slippery and as oddly inculpable as doom. I always thought that it mattered grievously that they were not south-ern, that perhaps the authorities catered to them because they weren't—as if we were trying to prove something egalitarian about southern justice to outsiders who might suspect our inclination to pro-tect our own. But this was the view from my blind side, as if Coy were truly considered one of us.

Over the years I continued to ponder Mary Smith's lie and I won-dered if, wherever she was, she felt remorse. Did she know that her accusation had led to Coy's untimely death? What sort of life had she lived after leaving Greensboro? Had she felt any compulsion, as she matured, to atone for her grave misjudgment, or having once gotten away with murder, had she developed a taste for it—perhaps at some corporate or political level? I wanted to confront her as an adult and discover that she had paid some price for her bad deed. Several dec-ades after Tom Doodley's death, my father had been called into the hospital emergency room to examine a patient who turned out to be the hit-and-run driver, a wretched alcoholic dying of liver cirrhosis.

Mary Smith's lie affected me. The first serious piece of short fiction that I ever wrote was the story of Coy's accusation and death, just as I have reported it here, probably more essay than fiction—a grandly di-dactic piece that found its only appreciative audience in the libertarian sixties. The story won a prize—an inscribed silver platter—when I was in college. The platter still sits on my china rail, tangible proof of this haunting.

My sense of the injustice that demolished Coy came as much from the girl I was brought up to be as from any proof that Mary Smith lied. There was no proof. What if she hadn't lied and Coy did what she accused him of doing? What if I suspected, as a fledgling writer, that without the lie there would be no story?

It's difficult to trace the origins of one's inspiration, but a large number of serious writers living and working today will attest to the fact that autobiography plays some part in determining the nature of their fictional interests. You are, simply, what you know, what you've experienced firsthand or vicariously, what you've read, thought about, dreamed, suppressed. In one way or another, how a writer has lived his or her life leaks out into the pages of what he or she writes in an array of oblique admissions: as atonement, self-condolence, apology, revenge, celebration.

In my own work, I would say that an autobiographical *attitude* persists, even if characters and the situations they find themselves in are conjured from thin air. Sometimes I might base a character on a piece of my own behavior that doesn't quite fit the puzzle of myself. I don't mean to suggest that the fiction I write pursues self-examination or analysis. If that were the case, readers would be bored to tears. If I drew you a picture of my psyche, it would look about as sophisticated as Mrs. Potatohead's.

I am essentially an optimist—which means that I come from a long line of potatoheads—and I probably write my fiction out of a need to understand this optimism, which is frequently more and more out of sync with a troubled world. It's not that I'm obtuse. It's not that I don't see the gloom. It's that I'm determined to throw it off and get on with whatever decency and pleasure remain obtainable. And so it is this stubborn desire to distract myself from the abominations of life, to circumnavigate them, that sustains my outlook and informs my fiction, fool of a potatohead though I may be. Beyond optimism, I am influenced by my personal struggles to ascertain the mechanics of justice in the world, bear witness to its triumphs and defeats and compromises. Recollecting my long writing life—which truly did begin when I was a child—I see that the theme of justice was something that fascinated me early and propelled my imagination. In his parable "The Three Boxes," about the origins of race and the divisive burdens of skin color, Fred Chappell describes justice as "the one thing in the world worth knowing that can be learned in the world and is not divinely revealed."

Something about the way my parents whispered about Mary Smith after they thought we children were asleep advised me that the whole truth had not been told. Something about the lack of commiseration shown Mary by other children at school suggested that their parents, as well, were mumbling suspicions. Something that I knew for myself about the ruinous ability of children who were loved and protected to glibly tell lies (because it was impossible for such children to believe that they wouldn't be forgiven) turned me powerfully against Mary. She took her place—representing my generation—in a long historical line of victimizers and deceivers, another version of the hit-and-run driver who had killed Tom Doodley long ago.

But a writer remembers the past with a memory that is sieved with the self-serving loopholes of revision. And the stories that are most seductive to the writer of fiction are often the ones that lack proof. Lack of proof gives one creative latitude. A writer remembers, glosses, improves, tells the truth as he or she calls it. But truth is childishly twitchy. It's like somebody you ask to sit still, to hold a particular position while you find the button on your camera, quickly, before the light changes. You saw a glimmer of something that was possible, but now truth has moved and the angle is not what you want and doesn't serve you as well.

More than plots, more than the battles between lies and truth that anger or enlighten, it's probably what a writer can never know with any certainty that inspires invention and inquiry. Why would a well-loved and happy little girl like Mary Smith lie? Was she indeed as happy as she seemed? It's always the question—not the answer—that makes you turn the page. Did the drunken fool who killed Tom Doodley mean to? Why weren't my parents or Mr. Helberg more outspoken in defense of Coy? Why did Coy give up without a fight? It's as if he lay down in a ditch and let himself be run over.

"Those were wonderful, happy years at Sternberger," Mr. Helberg said when I phoned him to inquire about the Mary Smith event. It was clear that he preferred to reminisce about the achievements of those times. "Do you remember that even back in the 1950s at Sternberger we taught conversational French? Typing? Bridge?"

"Yes sir," I said. "In fact, Sternberger is where I learned to type with four fingers—which is how I still do it." Mr. Helberg chuckled. I had

never seen him chuckle when I was a kid at his school. He was stern
and humorless and often grouchy, and only the bravest of us called
him Mr. Hamburger behind his back.

"Do you remember that we had a covered bicycle shed?" His voice
sounded as bright as a boy's. "On any given day, there were one hundred bicycles parked in that shed—without locks."

"One of those bikes was mine, Mr. Helberg," I said.

"Do you remember that we had an art teacher and a music
teacher?"

"Mrs. Crimm and Mrs. Bachtel. I remember everything."

"Do you also remember, Marianne, that your old sourpuss principal, David T. Helberg, played the violin?"

"Yes I do," I conceded. "It was a wonderful time."

Whose robe did we find in my grandfather's trunk, after my grandmother died—the grandmother who saved Tom Doodley's chickens.
My mother and I were sifting through their belongings, determining
what to keep, what to throw away. There in a leathery trunk with a
rusty latch, beneath moth-eaten blankets, old letters, a diary my grandfather carried during World War I, we uncovered a Klansman's robe
and hood. Rust stains bled from the metal fasteners and dirtied the
fabric. We unfolded the robe and held it up to the window light,
amazed, horrified, nearly speechless, questioning its authenticity. On
the breast of the robe was emblazoned the telltale scarlet cross.

"What's this doing here? Whose on earth is it? Why was it saved?"
my mother cried.

"Why was it *hidden*?" I asked.

"It's much too small to have belonged to your grandfather," she said
with relief. "It would only fit a child. Maybe it was a costume—for a
play or something."

"Nobody back then would have made one of these for a kid to wear
in a play—would they? What sort of play?"

"Let's ask your father. Maybe he wore it."

"Are those rust stains or blood?"

"All I know is that it couldn't possibly be your grandfather's robe—unless he wore it as a child."

"Maybe it was Grandmother's."

"They were both tall people," my mother said and sighed, folding the robe. "There's bound to be a reasonable explanation. Marianne, until we know what it is, please don't write about this, okay?"

But a writer can't stop writing simply because personal mysteries remain unsolved or incriminating or lies cleave irreconcilably to the truth. Never believe that lies are the flip side of truth; they are a clammy version, the rock bottom of a deep and airless place, the first ironic toehold, if we are persistent, in our climb upward and into fresh light.

Kinds of Trouble

ONE SUNDAY MORNING in June, right after church as we stood in the driveway still dressed in our pristine Easter outfits, I pointed to a ditch filled with weeds and I said to my brother Knothead, "I dare you to rub those weeds all over your arms and face." I must have been seething over something he'd said or done. I must have wanted to kill him. It was a frequent impulse.

"Okay," he said. "Why?"

"Because I dare you to."

He broke off a stalk of leaves and smelled them.

"Rub them all over yourself," I said.

"Okay," he said and did.

"Don't put any in your mouth though."

He tore off a single leaf, sniffed it, popped it into his mouth and chewed.

Knothead bragged that he loved all things that other kids hated: typhoid shots, okra, maggots, slugs. He liked smelling the stink of dead animals and picking them up with his bare hands. He liked Sunday school. At Sunday school he could tease the girls and get away

with it because the teachers were parent volunteers and probably tried
to pray bad behavior away rather than discipline it. He said he loved
casseroles—nobody but mothers loved casseroles. He braved the occasional bee sting with the shrugging aplomb of somebody who'd just
stubbed a toe. The only time he cried profusely was when he listened
to a popular song called "The Little White Cloud That Cried." He'd
turn up the radio and crawl up on the ledge of the bathroom sink to
observe himself in the mirror. The more he listened and watched himself, the more he perfected his agony. The sadder his facial contor-
tions, the harder he sobbed.

He said that if he were a convicted criminal sentenced to die, he
would choose the electric chair over the gas chamber. *Nobody* in their
right mind would have chosen the electric chair, but Knothead was
the sort of kid who liked sticking Mother's bobby pins into electrical
sockets to try to shock himself on purpose. He liked to electrocute his
mouth by chewing tinfoil. He went to sleep in the dental chair when
Dr. Pringle drilled his cavities. He claimed that Indian burns felt good
and that he liked to be frogged hard on his upper arms. All of his
boasts made you want to find his Achilles heel and drive a nail into it.

Above all else he loved dares, and the more challenging the better:
dares that might hurt him or test the true boundaries of his courage,
which as far as anyone could determine, were intergalactic in scope.
Daring him to rub weeds all over himself had assured his coopera-
tion. He was a master of self-sabotage.

"You're going to be so sick," I gloated.

"It's just leaves."

"Oh no it's not. Don't you know how to tell poison ivy from other
weeds?"

"I'm not allergic to poison ivy," he said, "so hahaha yourself."

"Just in case, I'd go take a bath real quick if I were you."

He waded into the infested ditch and plopped down in a tangle of
poison ivy and rolled around, mashing the leaves all over himself.
"Lahdeedahdeehoo!"

He came down with the worst case of poison ivy in our family's
history. He looked paved in pink pebbles, worse than the boy with

smallpox I was always daring myself to look at in my father's medical textbook, *Holt's Diseases of Infancy and Childhood.* He had blisters on his eyelids, inside his ears, his lips, the roof of his mouth, the whites of his eyes, even under his fingernails. He lay in a darkened room for days, mummified in gauze folded over applications of Calamine lotion. Daddy almost put him in the hospital. If he told on me, I'm sure my parents chastised him for going against his own common sense. Even if he'd forgotten what poison ivy looked like, what was he doing rubbing leaves of *any* kind on himself when he still had on his good church clothes? He survived the illness, of course; it may have been my first inkling that, like B'rer Rabbit, he was just saucy enough to always land on his feet and remain invincible. Still, as his manipulative older sister, I believed it incumbent upon me to sober him with inklings of his own mortality, and it wasn't long before another opportunity to do so presented itself.

On rare occasions when it snowed more than a few inches and schools were canceled, Starmount Country Club permitted kids to sled on the golf course hills. We owned one sled, and instead of arguing over who got to use it, I agreed to take Knothead up to the golf course and promised him we'd share. My plan was to ditch him as soon as we arrived.

It was bitter cold, and we dressed poorly for such weather. We never got enough snow to make buying proper cold-weather gear Mother's priority. Our winters tended to be so short and mild that by February jonquils and hyacinths bloomed. We wore heavy wool carcoats, easily sodden. We wore thin rubber boots over three or four pairs of our father's nylon socks. We wore socks for mittens, too. At best, dressed as we were, we could only stave off the early twinges of frostbite for two or three hours.

Preliminary frostbite felt like a buzzing in the toes of your boots. You'd push on a bit until the buzzing sharpened to a needling sensation. Afterward, you imagined that your legs were bolted mercilessly to blocks of ice, not feet. The feeling was of an aching, ironclad weight, and your shinbones thrummed as if the marrow had solidified.

The older kids were allowed to build a bonfire at the top of the steepest sledding hill at Starmount. You had to stand precariously near the flames for the snappish warmth to do you any good. Knothead was already complaining about the cold by the time we reached the country club and headed for the bonfire.

Who might have been at Starmount for me to pal around with? Most likely Bob Zane, whose distinction at school was being able to flip his eyelids inside-out and they'd stick that way until he decided to unfasten them; the Eldridge twins, who hostessed spin-the-bottle parties in their basement; Carolyn Dees, my best girlfriend, who introduced me to Johnny Mathis records and taught me the word "depressed." I'm certain Janet Turner was there, kindly shepherding her younger brothers, and Wayne McNairy, the neighborhood bully, ramming his sled at whoever made eye contact with him. Once I took up with my friends, I forgot about Knothead, guiltlessly.

It wasn't until I shuffled my frostbitten feet in the direction of the bonfire a couple of hours later that I remembered him. He was sitting on a log, close to the fire, hunkered down in his coat, shivering. "You can have the sled now," I said. He'd lost his hat. His ears and cheeks were chafed red from wind and cold. His runny nose was as pale and stiff as a parsnip, and he was sucking his thumb.

He was probably eight or nine years old, yet he still sucked his thumb when he felt in the need of comfort. People teased him about it, but he didn't care. In a way, I admired him for not caring what people thought, but thumb-sucking was just one more of his grotesque personal habits that dismayed me. I pretended I didn't know him and slumped down on a log on the opposite side of the fire. The warmth was hypnotic, and I stuck my boots as close as I dared.

It wasn't long before an older boy tapped my shoulder. "Little girl," he said, "I think your boots are on fire."

And they were: my red rubber good-for-nothing boots were smoking at the toes. I jumped up and stomped out the flames. The fire had melted gaping holes in the bottoms of both boots.

"We'd better start home now," I called to Knothead. "I've burned up my boots."

He nodded, his teeth chattering. "I'm f-f-freez-z-zing," he said.

"Where's your hat?"

"Wayne McNairy stole it."

"Where are the socks you wore for gloves?"

"In the creek."

"Oh for heaven's sake."

"Would you go find them for me?"

"Just forget about the socks," I told him. "Stick your hands in your pockets and let's go."

"Will you pull me on the sled?"

"All right, for a little while," I agreed. "Just stop acting so pitiful. I'm cold, too, you know. I've got holes in my boots."

He heaved himself onto the sled and I began to drag him uphill toward the road. It was the heaviness of his ingratitude that did me in. "Get off a minute. I can't pull you up something this steep," I told him.

"Can't move," he said weakly. "F-f-freez-z-zing. Can't feel my feet any more. Can't feel below my knees. P-p-paralyzed."

"Stop being melodramatic," I said. It was something our mother was always telling one of us.

I persuaded him to roll off the sled and hobble alongside me to Holden Road. We'd cross Holden to Starmount Drive, then I'd try to pull him the mostly level four blocks to home. I wasn't the least bit alarmed that his lips were turning blue. All summer he'd stay in the swimming pool until his lips turned blue, and no amount of cajoling could get him to leave the water until he was good and ready.

We crossed Holden on foot, but instead of hopping back on the sled, Knothead collapsed and, slowly, like a bandit shot off a horse, rolled down an embankment and lay spread-eagle in a snowdrift at the base of a tree.

"Why'd you go and pull a stunt like that?" I shouted. "I'm counting to ten, and if you haven't climbed back up here and gotten on the sled, I'm leaving without you."

Snowbaby, he say nuthin'.

I scooted down the embankment and mushed over to where he sprawled. "Why are you acting like this? Get up. Now."

We all knew from reading *The Call of the Wild* that people freezing to death got sleepy first. "Get up you big faker." I kicked his boot with my own. "You've made it impossible for me to rescue you."

"You're mean," he said. "Can't you see that I'm going into a coma?"

"Here. Hold out your arm and I'll pull you up."

"I can't. I don't have the strength to lift my baby finger. You'll have to carry me."

I bolted away from him and stomped up the hill. "Help me!" he croaked, but I did not look back until I'd marched nearly a block. I thought by then he would have tired of lying there without an audience. But I could see him, spread out flat on his back, probably sucking his thumb.

I kept walking. I reasoned that I'd done all that God could reasonably expect from me; after all I was only human. I had holes in my boots and by the time I'd limped home, it felt as if I had anvils for feet. I didn't worry about deserting Knothead or killing him. I had the perfect alibi. He'd refused to come home when I'd said it was time, been wholly uncooperative. It was, in its own warped little selfish knot of rationale, the perfect murder: the victim had played the role of my accomplice.

When I arrived home, I filled a pot with tepid water and soaked my frozen feet. I changed into clean warm clothes. I read *Bartholomew and the Oobleck* to my six-year-old brother, then I painted my fingernails. Not until I reposed on my bed, listening to WCOG broadcasting rock-and-roll from the radio tower above the Pig and Whistle Restaurant, did I remember Knothead. He'd gotten me into serious trouble at the Pig and Whistle when we were much younger. He'd pointed out a sailor, eating in the restaurant, whose forearms were profusely illustrated with tattoos. We'd ogled and laughed and chanted the melodious word "tattoo" in such singsong delirium that our parents had jerked us into our coats halfway through dessert. We were driven home in pounding silence and memorably spanked.

Knothead had the power to enlist me in enterprises of excessive mischief. In later years I would learn that the word for his magnetism was *charisma*. The word would seep into the culture when John F. Kennedy ran for president, but newscasters wouldn't commonly employ it until then. *Wily* was the word that existed before *charisma* upstaged it with its glossy, shameless, captivating, sly, seductive charm. Knothead got us into trouble because he could never outfox our parents. His strategies were wrong. But he didn't mind being wrong—that was the dirty trick of it. I minded being wrong. Being wrong made me feel shrunken and grave. But Knothead thrived on wrongness. It was a kind of heart's fuel for him. Was it a decisive difference between boys and girls of my generation that girls minded being caught at badness because the culture exalted their potential so highly? Girls were often discouraged against pursuit of immediate gratification. Were boys encouraged to be wrong as part of adventures in failure that would toughen them for manhood? Being wrong sullied a girl's potential, and heaven forbid a girl without potential. Because of her potential—cherished like a nest egg of goodness—a girl's life seemed composed of a series of postponements. Boys lived more gloriously, like animals, in the present zoom of instinct and sensation. It's why they didn't mind filth and loud explosions, and it's why they *expected* to wreck their bikes. Boys did everything as if they had nine lives.

The day I abandoned Knothead in the snow, I felt as if I was shucking myself of all sorts of trouble: the troublesomeness of a tagalong, a windbag know-it-all, an oblivious loudmouth phony baloney. It was as if I'd left a splotch of bubonic plague to freeze to death in the snow, not a brother. Everywhere I turned there was evidence of his contagion: not a single deck of playing cards in our house was complete because Knothead was forever clipping them to his bike spokes to make puttering engine sounds and disappearing the cards permanently; the volume control knob was missing from the television because Knothead had unscrewed it; the piano keys were sticky from his banging because he never washed his hands and because he ate atomic fireballs (jaw breakers that changed colors) and he was always taking the fireball out of his mouth and studying his blue green or red teeth in the mirror and rolling the fireball around in his fingers; he routinely used my toothbrush on his own mossy teeth; at breakfast he'd swipe my orange juice when his glass was empty; he'd beg and

beg for a favor, and if I relented, instead of saying thank you, he'd
bleat out a laugh and chant, "I get my own waaa-aaay, I get my own
waaa-aaay."

The truth was that because he could wrangle his own way so reli-
ably, he was a survivor. I didn't really believe that I'd left him to die in
the snow. I'd left him to *almost* die, or to be scared into thinking he
might die, the sort of suffering through which he could discover a
measure of resourcefulness and humility. As daylight began to fade,
I told myself that if he wasn't home by five o'clock, I'd bundle up
again and go out looking for him, even though I was vastly opposed to
missing the *Mickey Mouse Club*.

I lamented not having a watch that worked. Knothead had ruined
my Cinderella watch by wearing it in the bathtub. Drying it out in the
warming oven, my mother had cooked its innards and scorched the
exquisite figure of Cinderella in her ballgown. Now she looked like
a filthy chimney sweep. But I didn't need a watch to tell me that
evening was seeping a dusky gloom into the sky. Tracks in the yard
filled with shivery indigo shadow. Trees raked ice-scabby twigs against
a cooing sky. I was grateful to be inside.

"Where's Knothead?" Mother asked, cracking my bedroom door.

"I guess he's still playing outdoors," I said breezily. How could I
have? She held a wooden spoon coated with chocolate.

"I'm making brownies," she said. "I thought he'd want to lick the
platter." The platter was what we called the leftover goo in the mixing
bowl. Usually she gave me the stirring spoon to suck and Knothead
swabbed out the platter with his fingers.

"I'll lick the spoon *and* the platter this time," I said.

"Look," she said, pointing out a window. "Who are those boys?
What in the world?"

Two tall boys, Harris Pearce and Tommy Adams, junior high boys
I barely knew, blazed a trail across our yard. They'd linked arms to
form a pack-saddle, and slouched between them, riding more like royalty than baggage, sat Knothead, triumphant. I saw his mouth moving—he was probably giving them orders—but when Mother and I
opened the front door, Knothead drooped his head and pretended to
be unconscious.

The boys introduced themselves and unloaded him on to the living room sofa. He rolled out of their arms in a lump. "Where on earth did you find him?" Mother asked, stroking his frosty brow. I held my breath. I thought they were going to say that they'd found him niched in a gargantuan snowdrift and that he'd informed them that his cold-blooded sister had abandoned him to die. Instead, they said that they'd met him sitting around the bonfire and that, accidentally, he'd burned holes in both his boots, so they'd offered to carry him home.

"Poor little tyke," my mother grieved.

"I burned holes in my boots, too," I said, "and nobody carried me home." But nobody paid any attention and while Knothead thawed and pinkened, my mother sent me to fetch a pot of tepid water and allowed him to soak his feet right there in the living room, enthroned on the pea-green sofa with its twists of fancy fringe and the Currier and Ives print of cows wading in a pond hanging like a lovely dream of summer above us. Then Mother asked me to take the pan of brownies out of the oven to share with the good Samaritan boys, at which point Knothead rallied. He asked if she'd saved him the platter, and, of course, because of his timely arrival (and because his constant good luck ordained it), she had.

Once a girl named Sylvia Hobbs punched my friend Sandy in the face and gave her a bloody nose. A gang of us chased Sylvia home on our bicycles and held her hostage all day while her parents were at work, riding our bikes in a circle of savagery around and around her house, shouting insults, calling her Sylvia *Hoggs,* pitching dirt clods at the windows. It was the sort of trouble we excelled at—loud, barking, fangs-bared trouble. We fumed around, banging, slamming, halting our bikes with screeching brakes, leaving long black lashes of burnt rubber on the street. Our hearts felt justifiably armored in spikes. Hate and vindication were one and the same. Anger was nothing to fear or be ashamed of: it was simply the smokestack on the roofs of our brains, puffing away, venting. "Shut up." "Make me." "I hate your slimy guts." "Ditto." "I'm rubber, you're glue, everything you say bounces off me and sticks to you."

A child's trouble was concrete, immediate, and almost always confrontational. It was rarely brooded into existence. It hatched wildly and with flair. You could pick it up like a stone and throw it. The only trouble you were powerless against was some disease. Down the street the Ozmer baby had died from leukemia. Roy Rogers and Dale Evans had a Down's syndrome child who died. But normally, trouble was a survivable, clear-cut ordeal and manifested itself in some person you disliked, a rained-out parade, a punishment, minor injuries, a teacher's reprimand, an injustice wrought by bullies, the death of a pet, or a tack somebody placed in your chair. Child trouble seemed to have a finite quality that adult trouble lacked.

I observed that adult trouble hovered, was slow to drop its landing gear and settle in one spot. It revealed itself in flickers of expression, whispers, sly innuendoes designed to make an eavesdropping child lose interest. If child trouble was the brick you hurled through the window of a haunted house, adult trouble was the vaporous ghost rumored to be lurking inside.

One afternoon, Mrs. Babcock, a neighborhood friend of my mother's, dropped by. She was a small, intense squirrel-faced woman with a high, whiney voice. "I hope your mother's at home," she said as I opened the door. She darted a delving look past me, already shaking and collapsing her umbrella and shuffling her little shoes on the welcome mat. As soon as she glimpsed my mother in the hallway, she burrowed past me and grabbed my mother's hands as if for balance. "Thank goodness you're here. I have to talk with you," she said—and with such whispered desperation I knew I had to make myself scarce. I knew from watching the television dramas that my mother loved to watch: *Lux Video Theater, Schlitz Playhouse of the Stars, Death Valley Days*—"brought to you by Twenty Mule Team Borax"—and the *Loretta Young Show,* dramas that my mother claimed were too old for me and that sometimes made her teary. After watching Loretta twirl through the doorway in her diaphanous dress to introduce the program in which she would star, and after I'd watched it—most often a painfully tender love story—I thought I'd gleaned the prize adults were hoarding: fairy tales were fine for children to read, but only adults were permitted the chance to live them.

Perhaps it was Mrs. Babcock's flamboyant swirl into our house that made me think that her troubles had to do with love. I sensed that she was on the verge of tears and that my mother didn't want her to feel embarrassed by my audience. My mother entwined an arm around her and ushered her into the living room, and for the better part of the afternoon they spoke in hushed tones punctuated by little parachute puffings of Kleenex being drawn from a box and Mrs. Babcock blowing her nose.

"What's wrong with Mrs. Babcock?" I asked later, and of course my mother said that nothing was wrong, just some personal trouble, none of my business certainly.

"But she was crying."

"Well, I'd cry, too, if I were in her shoes," my mother huffed. But that was all she said, and the matter of Mrs. B's distress disappeared into the deepest chamber of my mother's steel vault of a heart.

In a week or so Mrs. Babcock returned for more counseling. Once again, she and my mother huddled in the living room whispering, Mrs. B intermittently blowing her nose. Crying adults meant serious situations. Crying female adults, however, often implied a vulnerability that couldn't be articulated. My mother cried more often and freely than my father. I'd only seen my father cry twice: at his father's funeral and when he watched the movie *Shane.* My mother cried over tender feelings provoked in her by weddings or a children's choir. She cried during emergencies as well. Once when she was giving my brother David a ride on the back of my horse-size Murray bicycle, he stuck his bare foot in the moving spokes and nearly cleavered off his heel. She cried so hard that she couldn't dial my father's office; a neighbor had to do it. She cried when she opened my father's Christmas gifts. The sweetest gestures, paradoxically, undid her. With my father, sadness was a hard thing he squinted at and fought. He did not want to cry in the movie *Shane,* when Alan Ladd rode away. Sniffling, he speculated that he was coming down with a cold. For Mother, sadness was a plush, wallowing submission she did not deny herself. It was the same with Mrs. Babcock, and maybe most women.

"Well, I wouldn't put up with it another day, if I were you," my mother advised her friend sternly. Easy for her to say; she wasn't in Mrs. B's shoes. Women displayed their fiercest and most puffed up selves when they gave other women advice.

From my child's perspective, Mrs. Babcock's ongoing distress suggested that she was trying to learn how to put up with trouble endlessly because she was clueless about how to squelch it. Whatever her situation, I thought, it wasn't nearly as bad as the persistent fact that she couldn't define the limits of her endurance.

~&

My friend Lily didn't care that her father was gruff, that he always looked uncomfortable, as if he suffered from heartburn or his clothes were too tight. Broderick Crawford looked that way on *Highway Patrol*. Mr. A looked uncomfortable even slopping around the house in an old bathrobe. He was rarely at home when I spent the night over there. He was working late at his hosiery mill, Lily said, or traveling, or playing cards at the M & M Club downtown in the O. Henry Hotel. Lily said that the M & M stood for Men. But what did the other M stand for? More, Lily said. Men and More Men. The Men and Men Club. Lily's mother told us that we could play all over the house, but not in Mr. A's room. He had a bad back; he slept in his own bedroom with a special firm mattress on the bed, and we were forbidden to jump on it. But of course we did. We jumped on it so violently that one night the frame cracked. We set it back up as best as we could so that nobody would know until grouchy, overstuffed Mr. A crawled into it one night and it collapsed. We tumbled around with laughter at the thought.

Mrs. A's bedroom, painted a delicate shell pink, was furnished with twin beds, neatly made with quilted flowered coverlets. She is the only mother I ever knew who owned a vanity. The vanity had a small, kidney-shaped mirrored top and a skirt that matched the print of the coverlets. The vanity's surface glittered with languid heaps of jewelry. Little towers of uncapped lipsticks smelled as sweet as jam. The powder puff, the softness and size of a magnolia bloom, smelled like a bride's bouquet. Nestled among the atomizers, pots of cold cream, lotions, and emery boards was a teacup. Always one swallow of tea, as amber as perfume, remained in the cup. A squeezed lemon wedge curled as if asleep on the rim of the saucer alongside the tiny sodden pillow of a spent tea bag. I was enthralled with the notion of sipping tea while you groomed yourself. It seemed so ladyfied, something my child-harried mother would have never attempted. My mother would have never left an empty teacup for someone else to carry into the kitchen either. Even if it was the maid's day, my mother would have carried her own used teacup to the sink. But Mrs. A had descended from gentry. She'd been a southern debutante, waited on and pampered. A governor perched in her family tree, although nobody ever bragged about it. The history of her family's prominence idled elegantly in her background like an old ornate tea service, dusky with tarnish, too cumbersome for everyday use, but steadfastly there all the same.

There was something superabundant about the way Lily and her mother lived: the way they shopped and dressed and ate and nurtured themselves. Their radiant dispositions, their dark honey-blonde hair, thick and irrepressibly curly, their tanned skin, the warm, luminous hair that furred the peachiness of their skin, suggested a female vigor, a whole-grained, bursting beauty, that soared apart from the leaden weight of the rest of their family.

Lily wore her expensive clothes with precision neatness. She never spilled milk or paint on herself at school. The cuffs of her socks were meticulously turned, and she did not wear scuffed shoes. I yearned to copy her, to embrace her style. Now and again my mother treated me to a Junior Circle Shop dress too, but my dresses were always rumpled and their sashes came undone. It was Lily's lushness of being, her exquisite carefulness, not her clothes, that I wanted to duplicate. One year we bought matching red-and-green plaid lunch boxes, and mine was the one that got dented and always smelled sour.

Lily's house was filled with dark, chocolatey-smelling furniture, some of which had probably been enshrined in the Governor's Mansion. She owned the most beautiful curtains I have ever seen: thick, shiny chintz printed with swallowtail butterflies. The walls of her room were the buttery color of sunbeams. Her comforter was quilted and smelled like lilac sachet, not mothballs.

Mrs. A cooked *whole* spaghetti, not the chopped up spaghetti casserole my mother slung together made with ketchup and tomato soup instead of genuine sauce. Lily showed me how to wind long, sophisticated noodles, holding a soupspoon against my twirling fork. They poured milk on their Jell-O. They used the word "cupboard" rather than cabinet, "pantry" rather than broom closet, and Mrs. A said "Coca-Cola"—an entire undulating lullaby compared to the snippy way my family all said "Coke."

Even though I learned to ignore Lily's bully brother, and Mrs. A never raised her voice in anger, and whenever I did bump into Mr. A he called me "Blondie" and tousled my hair, in spite of feeling welcomed and sheltered in their house, I sensed a dire asymmetry. That Mrs. A slept apart from her husband, that they never kissed, seemed to tilt the house like an unbalanced see-saw, turn it topsy-turvy with this riddle: there was a man who wasn't at home, even when he was there.

There was also the sort of trouble that a child could see advancing that an adult pretended not to. At my friend Julie's house, I used to pray that her mother wouldn't attempt to make conversation with her father in the evening. We'd be setting the table when he drove under the carport, and Julie's mother would dart glances at both of us, as if we were two mirrors, and say, "Is my lipstick on crooked? Have I put on too much rouge? He hates it when it looks like I don't try." I thought that she tried mightily, and that's what he despised about her. She'd untie her apron, pick off any tidbits sprayed on her sweater from cooking. She waited at the back door for him, wide-eyed and with the absurd expectation that this time he would pay attention to her, even kiss her on the cheek. I'd never seen Julie's parents embrace; proximity repelled them. He barged past her every time, tossing his coat at her, which she caught like a good hall tree. Sometimes she trailed after him, only to be shut out. "Could I have some goddamn privacy in here, please Ann?" we'd hear him shout. She'd amble back to the kitchen with the cowed look of a scolded dog.

"I shouldn't have worn this sweater," she might say. "It's new. He hates for me to spend money on clothes. I don't know why he's like that, except that his own mother was such a tightwad." Or she might say something like, "I knew I shouldn't have cooked meatloaf tonight. Smelling it always puts him in a bad mood. I know that he doesn't like meatloaf, but it's just so easy and inexpensive to make." Or she'd say, "*Now* what did I do?" and beg us to guess.

I was tempted to say, "You exist." I believed that this was the only thing about her that he constantly resented.

We'd get through dinner just fine as long as Julie's mother didn't try to start a conversation. They didn't say the blessing. He bent over his plate and ate quickly, watching his food in a beady, vigilant way. Sometimes he might ask me, the guest, a terse question: "How's your family?" A question I could answer with one bland word: "Fine."

But after a while, Julie's mother agitated against any silence—especially a brooding one, especially one that hovered like a poisonous mushroom cloud. I hoped that she'd learn from past mistakes, but she didn't. She kept pushing him. "How did your day go?" she'd venture. "Are you in a bad mood?" "I read where it takes more muscles to frown than to smile," she'd say lightly, and I'd cringe. "Relax, Mr. Poker-face. Cheer up," she'd say.

It would end badly. But it was clear to me that Julie's mother picked these fights. She picked them to get him to notice her, to prove that she wasn't thin air. I was just a child, but I detected the futility. There was nothing to win, no happiness, no fresh start. They went around and around in endless cycles of goading and argument, no time-outs. Theirs was the longest trouble I ever observed without somebody breaking down in tears and calling it quits. They were past crying.

One of the privileges of childhood was that trouble seemed elective. It tended to follow a pattern of cause and effect, and you could often outsmart it, like twirling your bicycle around a pothole. Even the saddest children I knew believed that they teetered on the periphery of trouble, observing its flames, unsinged.

Childhood was the Land of Second Chances Forever. We were always beginning some strategy anew—our zest for doing so was inexhaustible. We bounced on failure like a trampoline; we never believed the worst. We surrendered our innocence gradually, in fits and starts, and a few of us will continue to do so all the days of our lives. Sometimes our starkest losses began mildly—as cracks rather than breakage, as infringements rather than deprivations. As much as any load of trouble, it was our capacity for reflection and self-examination that finally grew us up: when we relinquished hardheartedness, when we advanced respect for an idea we once disparaged, when someone we'd determined to avoid or trivialize, we came to cherish.

The shock for me was that I'd thought I wanted to prove that Knothead was as mortal as the rest of us.

One afternoon while tumbling around at a friend's house, Knothead fell. His playmate's mother judged the accident serious and brought him home. He seemed disoriented and in need of comfort, she said, and suggested that we watch him for signs of concussion.

Mother tucked him straight into bed. She questioned him about the mishap, but he couldn't remember what had happened. By the time our father arrived home, he felt nauseated and sleepy.

"We don't want you to go to sleep," Daddy told him.

"I want to. I'm so shoe."

"You want me to take your shoes off?"

"Turn the milk down please," he said, shutting his eyes tightly.

I thought he was faking. I thought he was trying to convince everybody that he'd hit his head falling and was now a victim of amnesia and had forgotten how to talk.

"What's your name?" our father asked kindly.

"Knothead Buie."

"What day is it?"

"Wednesday."

He was right about both.

"Do you feel sick?"

Knothead nodded, his eyes swimmy with tears.

"Point to where it hurts most."

He pointed all over his head.

"What's your street address?"

"109 Elgin hotdog."

My younger brother, David, and I bleated with laughter. We hovered over the bed like curious onlookers at the scene of a wreck.

"Do you remember playing at Vic Cocheran's this afternoon?" Daddy asked in a somber voice.

"We pumped on the jed. We bayed appleball. My green hurts. I don't want to talk any feathers. I want to go to lamp. Take off my horse and turn out the beans."

"I'd better take this boy to the hospital," Daddy said. "He's aphasic. Do we know for sure whether he fell and hit his head? I don't feel any unusual lumps."

"His entire head is lumps, but that's normal," Mother said. "Oh dear, what's wrong with my little Knothead?"

"Mommy, I'm rusty," he said. "Could I have a sup of nostrils?"

"*Nostrils!*" David and I cackled, and Daddy glared at us.

"Are you thirsty? Do you want a cup of water?" Mother translated. He nodded weakly.

"Better not have anything to drink right now," Daddy said. "Let's go, buster." He helped slide Knothead into a jacket and promised he'd phone Mother directly from the emergency room.

I remember how small and benign Knothead looked as Daddy folded him into his arms. Mr. Bigmouth so shrunken and waifish, pressing his aching noggin against the lapels of Daddy's coat, burrowing, wanting so much to go to sleep, sucking his thumb.

Then Daddy hoisted him. It made me sad to see him carried. I rubbed his back and laid my cheek against it and kissed him, too. We all did.

I couldn't eat supper. I excused myself from the table and walked

outside on the front porch. The neighbors' chihuahua ran around in
their yard and barked. Why wasn't there something wrong with that
damn dog's head? That's what I was thinking. Why was he allowed to
run around making a nuisance of himself while poor Knothead was
laid out flat on a gurney? He was a terrible, mannerless, idiotic dog. If
you went over there to visit and set your pocketbook beside a chair,
the chihuahua would sniff it out, cock his leg, and urinate as if your
purse were a fire hydrant. Why didn't some ill fate waylay him?
When, if ever, had I told Knothead that I loved him? *Did* I love him,
or was I scared that a hole had been blown in the shelter we called
family and that now, one by one, we would be unceremoniously
sucked out? Maybe the universe had decided that we'd been lucky
long enough.

Mother came out on the porch to join me, draping one arm around
my shoulder and pulling me close. I could smell the fragrances of the
supper I hadn't eaten embedded in her clothing. "They're keeping
him overnight," she said. "He may have an aneurysm. They'll do tests
first thing in the morning."

"What's an aneurysm?"

"It's a weak spot in a blood vessel, sort of like a weak spot in a tire."

"Can they fix it?"

"Sometimes. It depends where it's located in the brain."

"He's going to have *brain* surgery?" It sounded Frankensteinish,
as close to hopelessness as my family had ever slunk. "Could he *die?*"

My mother squeezed my shoulder. This may have been the first
question I'd ever asked her that she didn't have a ready answer for.
"We'll know more when all the tests are finished," she said. "No use
second-guessing. Aren't you going to eat your supper?"

But I couldn't eat; it would have felt sacrilegious to be hungry at a
time like that. I felt too rusty to eat.

Late that same night, I heard my father come in and I crept into
the hallway to hear what he was saying to Mother. He was describing
the sorts of tests Knothead would undergo. In one test, dye would be
injected into the spinal cord to darken veins and blood vessels so that
doctors could pinpoint swelling. In another test, a bubble of air would

be instrumental in determining neurological abnormalities. I heard my mother crying. It was the thunderous sound of a mountain collapsing, an avalanche of grief. It was a different kind of crying than I'd ever heard before: not panicky or sentimental or self-pitying, but raging. Her tears weren't self-promotional like Mrs. Babcock's. They were tears wept from her marrow that the Red Cross might have used, like blood, to save a life.

I tossed restlessly, falling in and out of sleep, waiting to hear the phone ring in the middle of the night, some official summoning us to the hospital where my brother's aneurysm had ruptured. I envisioned the aneurysm as delicate, trembling and tear-shaped, clinging to the steep slope of a vein, a frail, membranous sackload of tears. When I said my prayers, I offered up my new thoroughbred horse as sacrifice if God would postpone Knothead's heavenly departure. If it turned out that Knothead had an inoperable aneurysm, one he might live with for a while, I would sell Golden Wonder immediately and buy two clunky old pleasure horses: one for Knothead, one for myself. We'd go riding everywhere together, seeking pleasure all during the last days of his life. To seal the bargain, I announced it to my parents in the morning.

They expected me to go to school, act normal, go to my piano lesson in the afternoon at Mrs. Lake's, three houses up from ours. Mother would call Mrs. Lake's house from her vigil at the hospital to give me a progress report. Now that I'd been told the worst, treated like an adult, I was expected to be brave like one. It was not the privilege I'd anticipated. My worry that Knothead suffered was a bramble of knowledge that I had to hack myself through all day. What did I care that I'd forgotten to bring lunch money? Who needed to eat when their brother was probably dying? Did it matter that I hadn't studied for the English vocabulary test? I was probably the only student in class who could define "aneurysm." Who cared if Clayton Cleaves hadn't invited me to her make-out party?

I went into the girls' room every chance I got, to cry over Knothead. I told everybody I was sick with cramps, when I'd never had a cramp in my life—except maybe writer's cramp. I kept my anguish private and muffled. People in junior high school, even your best girl-friends, were too busy primping for anguish.

Mrs. Lake met me on the steps of her front porch. She was mar-ried to a surgeon and used to dealing with emergencies. Recently my baby brother, John, had gotten a chicken bone stuck in his throat. My father, carrying John, had dashed down to the Lakes' while my mother phoned. In transit, the bone dislodged, but Dr. Lake met my father on the front porch, ready to perform a tracheotomy with a paring knife.

I fell into Mrs. Lake's arms, sobbing while she smoothed my hair. It felt like I had a bone stuck in my heart.

"It's all right," she said at once. "Your mother called and he's okay. They didn't find an aneurysm. They think it was a concussion after all."

The relief was so immense that I cried harder.

"I'll bet you haven't practiced much," Mrs. Lake said. "Who cares, right? Let's don't have a piano lesson today, let's have a party. How about we make tea and sit in front of a fire and talk about your love life?"

And I giggled then, because I didn't have a love life—I was always lamenting that fact to Mrs. Lake—but I was the happiest girl in his-tory anyway, at that moment. I was happy for triumphant reasons, not superficial ones, and blessedly free from hate, pettiness, suspicion, dis-gruntlement, and all their attendant complaints and speculations. I was free to range among a million second chances, my girlhood still intact, granted a reprieve from the sort of comeuppances of fate that transform and subdue. It wasn't yet time for me to yoke myself to the loads of trouble that adults took on.

"We'll let somebody else take their piano lesson seriously today," my teacher said. "You just keep practicing."

My First Marriage

BY LATE OCTOBER, the balmy stupor of Indian summer had finally lifted. Nights chattered with the spiky roll of leaves and blown twigs and the scoot and puffery of wind torn loose from the North Star. Flies disappeared. The last of the cicadas clinked miserly like tiny china teacups dropping somewhere in the woods. Pasture grass was not so high that you might stumble down a hole walking out to catch a horse. Persimmons had fallen off the persimmon trees and the horses made clown faces eating them, curling their lips, nickering to one another as if to laugh off the filmy, puckering taste. At dusk, the sky dropped over the land like chilly blue silk, and the horses, snorting air that had turned into frosty tonic, frisked around the paddock, impatient to be fed.

The horses acted drunk with life, and why not? They were sated with good fortune: brisk weather, warm barn, pastureland and woods to roam, the velvetizing closeness of each other. We doted on them. We pretended that they loved us back, that in their suede-soft eyes we glimpsed tenderness and gratitude, but we knew otherwise. We forgave them their bad tempers, their indifference, because we were young girls, learning to please, and would some day want to love men and accommodate children, and the horses were teaching us how. We fed them orchard grass, clover, lespedeza hay, palmfuls of sweetfeed, timothy and alfalfa. We cracked the skim of ice off their water buckets with our bare hands and rode them without saddles or halters, holding onto their manes in a swoon of trust. We brushed them and sang to them and hung rapturously on their necks. We counted on their magic to soar us past ourselves.

I had sold my pleasure horse and bought Goldy, a thoroughbred and jumper, so that I could foxhunt and go to horse shows and win ribbons. I suppose I sold the pleasure horse because I'd grown bored with gentleness and wanted to be fancy. I was nearly fifteen. I was not as interested in pleasure anymore as I was in boys, but I still went up to Mr. Lambeth's barn every day after school to ride.

I'd taught myself how to ride when I was younger, mostly willing the knowledge out of desire and tenacity. I had a certain prescience about horses; I thought I understood their hearts. We all felt that way. We would have *been* horses if given the choice. It was an enthrallment, less like seduction than onslaught. We smelled like them, ran like them, bluffed like them, looked like them in our ponytails. We dipped handfuls of sweetfeed out of the bins and chewed it because it was theirs.

I remained shy around Goldy, daunted by her grandeur, her habits unpredictable and strange. I could not always control her, a truth that thrilled me in some lovesick way. Her willfulness suggested part of my own evolution toward a spiritedness that might wreck us.

Since the weather had cooled, she'd turned all the more glamorous, tossing her chestnut mane, snapping her tail to and fro. I knew better than to gallop a spitfire in the direction of home at feeding time. You galloped on your way out, but not on your way in, not on a horse that had been bred for racing.

We were jogging home that October afternoon, up Jefferson Road, when she spooked at something fluttering in the ditch, perhaps a

Dixie cup. Pam was riding Gay Girl, such a lady of a horse that she seemed to carry her saddle as primly as a pocketbook. Pam danced her politely out of our way while Sandy struggled to restrain Let's Go. Let's Go was all nerves, wall-eyed and huffy, and her neck, checked by a martingale, arched like a carousel pony's. Her turbulence was contagious, a signal to Goldy, who, like all beasts of burden, was essentially an opportunist.

The fluttering Dixie cup may have started the stampede, or Let's Go's influential derangement on the sort of brisk afternoon when the weather might have been blamed as well, cold air whipping horses' sassy flanks, dropping down their backs like tricks of ice. Whatever the cause of the runaway, it began. I was powerless to stop it, although I yanked and pleaded. When a horse goes haywire—and this happens suddenly, at any given moment, even to a horse you think you understand—you are too intent about hanging on to jump off. The more powerful reflex is to cling as you would to a runaway amusement-park ride.

Although she strained to follow, we passed Let's Go in a streak. She was too cantankerous and unfocused to compete. Scattering her energy in ornery skittishness, she preferred dervish to stride. Goldy was a strider, elongating as she ran. Her roiling speed, as oddly lilting as it was thunderous, felt sturdy and purposeful, not chancy. Once I gave into her, it was as if I rode in the eye of her storm. I lay as flat against her neck as her own two ears and accepted my diminishment, felt the streamlining effect of the wind purling by.

Up ahead I saw the split-rail fence that bordered posted land, and I knew that she would take it, that I couldn't stop her, that she bore me away like a magician performing a vanishing act. Indeed, she leapt the fence as if it were no taller than a weed, then headed into an opulence of unfamiliar grass and sky, advancing across a tilt of golden fields toward a distant row of dark trees shaped like flames.

In hues of blush and radiance, the whole sky rushed my face, or perhaps it was the tender color of my eyelids closed against a late-flung sun that throbbed against the vibrance of my tears, loosened by wind and fear and exultation. For we had both survived Goldy's leap, had we not?

Ahead unfolded a terrain that seemed to bloom away from itself, urgent to consume us. And if there were spaces between the cedars, I never saw them. I saw only the princely trees, tall and severe, a march of husbandry around this place, a landscape that addressed us like a formal suitor. The trees loomed almost watchfully, balancing silver epaulets of clouds on their fine shoulders. But the earth pitched toward us, not we to it. If I had been able to halt Goldy, I'm certain that the earth would have continued to unfurl beneath us, would have insisted on our trespass. Whiplike grasses drummed us along, and we raced full speed ahead. There were no more fences, but we prepared ourselves for ascent.

Up over one vertical cedar we soared, or possibly it bent and scooped us into its giant spade. I swear that's how it happened. We arrived, for an instant, at the zenith of my girlhood, transcendent, like true unfreighted love, wildly certain art, a two-star constellation, the ornaments atop a wedding cake.

Horses and Boys

IN THE SPRING of 1960, I boarded my first horse, Cherokee, at the Hill 'n' Dale Hack Shack. Burt Spruill owned the Hack Shack and managed it as a boarding facility and riding school. He was probably in his late thirties, divorced (or getting there), and frequently you could smell liquor on his breath. His style of management was that he was everybody's pal.

A group of teenage girls, older than I, hung out at the Hack Shack. A couple of them owned horses which they boarded there, but the majority had a more ambiguous purpose. They mucked out stalls for Burt Spruill and exercised his horses, and I don't think they got paid. They did the work because they were devoted to the place; my mother speculated that they did it because they were devoted to Burt.

They were lithe and fearless girls, the bravest riders I ever knew, utterly relaxed on horseback, their bones astutely floppy. Burt had taught them everything they knew about horses, and they rode with slit-eyed smugness, so confident that they looked sleepy. If a horse refused a jump and nearly threw them off, they sagged upon the horse's neck and laughed in its face. If they fell, they bounced nimbly upright from the dust, like fallen acrobats springing from a safety net.

When the girls weren't riding or shoveling out stalls, they enthroned themselves on bales of straw, telling dirty jokes. Or they
saddle-soaped tack. Or they leaned dreamily on fence posts and
sucked in the daze-making air of the place. They satisfied themselves
with simply being there.

I saw enthrallment in their faces when they talked to Burt. They
competed for his attention the way pupils of a favored teacher might.
But if any of them went slinking into the hayloft with him—as my
mother suspected—nobody bragged or cried or whispered about it.

I viewed them all as girls foremost in love with horses. Burt, who
owned some of the horses they loved, was their means of access. That
he was a cowboy and spoke their language, that he loved the horses,
too, and was keen around animals, even when he was drinking, made
him kindred. They thought of him, perhaps, as half-man and half-
horse. It would have been a natural extension of their love for the
horses if the girls had admitted Burt into their hearts as well. They
watched him stroke his ruddy man's hand down the neck of a troubled horse and listened raptly to his kindly, confidential voice, and
they believed in the sort of man who probably does not exist except
in lulls and snatches.

I never felt included in the camaraderie of the Hack Shack. I was
wary around Burt Spruill because of my mother's suspicions. I felt in-
timidated by the older girls, their daredevilry, their hotshot riding
skills, the sensual drapery they made of themselves whenever they
embraced a horse. When the weather turned steamy, they rode in their
bathing suits and Burt squirted them with a hose. They called manure "shit."

The stable itself was a squat, grubby shelter; there were tree stumps
in the yard that we used for mounting blocks. There were no riding
trails close by, no streams or woods. The surrounding land had the
exhausted, weedy look of lapsed maintenance. Above the barn and
riding ring slanted one small, bleak, briar-stubbled field that always
made me think of the fabled cemetery in old westerns, Boot Hill. If
you left the stable grounds and rode your horse along the narrow

shoulders of either Lawndale Drive or Battleground Road, you contended with heavy traffic. The Hack Shack property, squeezed by development, had no rural context. It was more of a hangout than a genuine farm, my mother said. She didn't approve of Burt's loose supervision. The name Hack Shack sounded sleazy, she said.

I wasn't yet thirteen—a totally guileless, stringy-limbed, horse-crazy tomboy. My notion of Paradise was spending a weekend with my girlfriend who lived on a dairy farm and rolling around in the silage. I had nothing in common with the Hack Shack girls who were on the verge of giving up their horses for men, who lit their cigarettes with big wooden kitchen matches that, now and again, they struck against one leg of Burt Spruill's tight jeans.

Yet my parents feared for my innocence. There was too much fecundity adrift at the Hack Shack: too much animal breath, cats birthing kittens in straw, the feverish copulation of green flies in dung. High up in the barn rafters, cobwebs floated as silkily as tossed-off lingerie. And so my parents made arrangements to board Cherokee elsewhere.

Normally docile, Cherokee was a stocky, compact, easily managed horse. The white blaze on his forehead, as bright and friendly as a search beam, gave him a bedazzled look. His shaggy fetlocks fringed tough, platter-shaped hooves that went unshod. Molasses-colored, with a blonde mane and tail, he gave evidence of having Belgian workhorse in his mixed-up blood. He was considered a pleasure horse because he never said no, but there he stood on moving day, a massive block of rootedness, telling Burt Spruill *No.* As Burt tried to tug him toward the horse transport, Cherokee snorted and balked. Resistance enlarged him. *No,* he would not clomp onto that strange little stall on wheels—and go where?

I interpreted Cherokee's fear as some awareness, similar to a wave of encroaching homesickness, that he was about to be parted from familiar ground. I imagined that tears glimmered in his eyes. When I stepped forward to comfort him, Burt briskly directed me out of the way and produced from his pocket the dreadful twitch.

It was a simple tool: a blunt wooden paddle with a cord of thick rope looped through one end. The rope lassoed an animal's top lip and, when twisted, cinched it. I watched as Burt applied the twitch while the dispassionate Hack Shack girls smacked Cherokee's flanks with sticks. "Get into the damn trailer, you son of a bitch," one of them snarled—and in front of my father.

I was nearly crying. I was years from experiencing an inkling of what the Hack Shack girls knew about timely assertions against brute force. They were not, these girls, in as much danger as my parents supposed; a precocious toughness carapaced their hearts, a toughness that would elude me for decades and only arrive in miserly increments. Perhaps this is what my parents knew about me: that I needed time to love my horse in my own sprawling and unprotected way and that they were moving us to a place where I could do just that—be a softhearted child for as long as I could, love my horse on my own silly terms, not anybody else's, humanize him, let him break my heart, make a fool of me with his orneriness. I was an eager, sacrificial kind of young girl. I could only learn to be master by first offering myself as slave. I would not be ready to move past my idolatrous love of a horse into other phases of rapturous preoccupation—writing poetry, painting, searching for a boyfriend—until, like the Hack Shack girls, I could view Cherokee as an obstacle and bully him out of my way with a stick.

Mr. Tom Lambeth, the retired owner of a Greensboro construction company, lived just outside the city limits on nearly fifteen acres of unspoiled countryside wedged between Westridge and Jefferson Roads. His vista included lawns as pampered as golf greens, sloping pastures, a scrubby field or two fringed by woods, flower and vegetable gardens, an arbor of scuppernong grapes, and down a sandy lane that led from his house and through a gate, a tidy red-and-white-painted Dutch Colonial barn with a corral. His farm was one of the last well-kept expanses of verdure between Greensboro and Guilford College.

Mr. Lambeth's own house, set back from Westridge among a huddle of shade trees, was an unaffected but spacious ranch with the assertive modern gaze of crank-style windows. The house had yellow shutters—a woman's sunny touch, I always thought, probably because Mr. Lambeth was so hard-boiled. But I do not recall meeting his wife and seem to remember that she was an invalid. The household was well tended by people in uniform: a cook, a maid, perhaps nurses bustled in and out. On occasion, when I needed to use the telephone and entered the back door as I'd been instructed to do, I observed a meticulous order. A spotless kitchen was always redolent of someone's supper preparations. Sometimes I spied a pie, set on a trivet to cool. Deep within the mahogany shadows of the house, I could hear a mantle clock ticking.

A young, neatly dressed handyman named Willie—polite in a simmering way, like Sidney Poitier—mowed the yard and fields, repaired fences, tended the garden, stacked firewood, and generally did whatever Mr. Lambeth required to ensure the farm's upkeep. Mr. Lambeth himself was done laboring. I suppose I believed he was a taskmaster, adept at barking orders and keeping his help busy. I never observed Willie lounging on a bale of straw, daydreaming like the Hack Shack girls.

Mr. Lambeth was a small, taut man with a flushed and veiny face. He had a full head of whitening hair that reared stiffly back from his tall forehead. He was slight enough to have been a jockey and gave the impression of having sat atop many a horse in the winner's circle. I recall that he wore jodhpurs, but I think it was his stance: slightly bowlegged and sporty. I never saw him ride a horse, nor did he own any animals. He smoked cigars, ventured not a syllable of small talk, carried a walking stick, possessed a skeweringly judgmental blue-eyed gaze. I was, of course, afraid of him. As a landlord, he loomed over the pleasure we took from his property as a kind of gentrified Oz.

I don't know why he opened his farm to us. He didn't need rental money. He could have kept its pastoral serenity intact. Perhaps he missed the commotion of his long-grown children. He had been a family man.

My father had found out about Mr. Lambeth's barn through a

patient whose daughter boarded her horse there. Stall and pasture
rental was $15 a month. We were required to order and pay for our
grain and hay and to share feeding duties with the other boarder.

❧

Assailed by the sweet languid fragrance of pasture grass and honeysuckle, my father and I drove together into Mr. Lambeth's kingdom
on the morning of our move. Burt Spruill's truck, towing the trailer on
which Cherokee had bravely borne his journey across town, rumbled
close behind. Mr. Lambeth was waiting at the pasture gate. Beyond
him unfurled acres of shining pastureland bordered by woods and
swamps of shade. A froth of wildflowers floated atop the tall grass,
and all manner of insects and birds swooped in giddy trajectory, as if
carrying love notes from one end of the land to the other. My impulse
was to leap out of the car before it stopped, to rush for the gate and
slip into that lush country, unimpeded by the nice skirt my mother
had insisted that I wear and the protocol of introductions. My mother
had wanted me to make a good impression on Mr. Lambeth, not to
appear to be too much of a ruffian.

A girl emerged from the woods as if she were a dream of my freed
self. She was my age, brown as cider, with a cap of ginger-colored sun-
lit hair. She wore shorts, a t-shirt, and holey sneakers without socks.
She was leading a plump black-and-white-spotted mare by a halter,
and she arced her free arm in a broad and friendly wave.

"That's Sunny," Mr. Lambeth said.

Burt Spruill had parked his truck, preparing to unload Cherokee.
I watched Mr. Lambeth sizing *him* up as a ruffian—I was glad I had
worn my skirt—then I moseyed over to the gate to talk with Sunny.

"It's a beautiful place you've got here, Mr. Lambeth," my father
said.

"Yes indeed," said Mr. Lambeth, puffing his cigar.

"Horse heaven," my father said, grinning at me.

"*Girl* and horse heaven," amended Sunny.

"That's right," said Mr. Lambeth. "Girl and horse heaven." He
swept the land with a proprietary gaze. He studied Sunny and me,

too, as if searching for proof that we had not misrepresented our intentions. We were a couple of good, trustworthy innocents, weren't we? He seemed to peer into our very hearts as if into arenas where fences might need mending or reinforcement.

"There's one rule here," he said. "No boys allowed."

Owning a horse—the physical requirements of such a venture—was an acceptable way for me to disengage from purely female things: skirts, perfume, stockings and garter belts, training bras, the prissy hygiene of shaved legs and tweezered eyebrows. To stomp around in a pair of loud muddy boots, to dig and shovel manure, to stink of horse sweat and the linseed oil we massaged into leather to keep it supple, to get rained on and not change clothes, to scoff at bedraggledness and keep wearing the wet jeans that rubbed against stirrups and pressed damp skids of chafing denim against your legs, to suck blood from an injury, to smash a horsefly with your bare fist, feel the sudden splatter of its putty innards, to watch a male horse urinate, to scale fly eggs out of a horse's mane, to detect the burning fruit-punch scent of a mare in heat, to get rubbed off on trees, stepped on, stung, bitten, to smack a switch against the flank of a beast ten times larger than yourself—these were not dainty enterprises.

I loved the rollicking dirtiness, the thin black rinds of filth under my fingernails, the way horse hair and sweat mingled and dried lacily on the insides of my calves and thighs, if I'd gone riding bareback. In summertime, we rode in shorts. If we used saddles, the stirrup leathers bruised and pinched our legs, leaving welts the size of raspberries. None of it hurt.

I once stepped into my mother's car—she was transporting a freshly baked pie to my grandmother—and planted one sludgy boot in the middle of the pie. It was clumsy of me, ruinous and knavish, but I laughed. What did a bit of nastiness matter? I was immune to the nitpickery of cleanliness and caution. I remember thinking that my mother was fussy not to try and salvage the pie. I would have eaten around the bootprint.

Time spent at the barn in the company of horses and dogs and field
mice and black snakes and spiders who strung webs the size of ham-
mocks and wanton stray cats who furtively dropped their litters in the
hayloft introduced me to the seductive righteousness of the vulnerable,
the brutal, the ugly and forgotten. In the livid flare of a horse's nostril
I glimpsed something as secretively visceral as an organ. My little
piano practicing palms grew callused. I could poke a dead bird with a
stick and not wince at the maggots stitching in and out. Time spent
breathing the smokeless smoke above fermenting piles of dung steep-
ing in warm grass (a scent not unlike the fragrance of my father's
whiskey sours) and time spent showboating, riding backward, sidesad-
dle, provoking Cherokee to buck me off, daring him, goading without
mercy, clanging against earth, landing in thorns and mud and jumping back on—this wild, lucky, violent rush toward life transformed
me into some dusty, wayward creature midway between child and
pest: part girl, part crust, more spit than dewdrop. I turned tawny,
shucked off my pearly indoors skin and tanned the colors of Cherokee
himself, the better to fuse with him and disappear. When I was at the
barn, I did not want to separate myself from a single mote or splinter
of it.

We rode rowdily, without helmets, cowgirls in English saddles
(mine was actually an old cavalry saddle that a relative had donated
to my horsey cause). Sometimes we mounted our horses from the rear,
at a run, then whooped across the big pasture as startled birds flapped
out of the weeds. We were still young enough to play gypsies or Indian girls. We made costumes and painted our horses and braided
their tails with feathers. When it snowed and schools closed, we'd
head for the barn with our sleds. Attaching them to our saddles with
long swags of rope, we'd journey into the suburbs to sell horse-drawn
sled rides to the kids.

Each summer morning, before the day grew hot, we took trail
rides. Beyond Mr. Lambeth's fences, woods and fields were plentiful.
We discovered an old logging path that twisted through vacant land
between Jefferson Road and Guilford College. There was a Phillips
66 station at our end of Jefferson. We'd stop off whenever we got

thirsty, hitching our horses to a picket fence, splurging on bottled drinks that were so cold they contained blades of amber ice. We cut branches off trees and fanned the flies away as we rode. We knew where there was a ravaged apple orchard, never harvested, and we took advantage of the fruit that bowed the tree limbs by midsummer. Our horses grazed whatever had fallen on the ground while we lolled on their backs in the buzzing shade, eating apples so tart they made our teeth chime. We took the horses swimming in the Guilford College Lake. The movement of a horse in deep water is the distinctly lilting up-and-down rhythm of a carousel animal. Up and down they pumped, with astonishment on their faces, snorting at the water, tricked into it but trembling with the thrill of buoyancy and cool. Their dung rose and bobbed plumply on the water's surface.

We investigated all open and wooded land, posted or unposted, within a five-mile radius of Mr. Lambeth's barn. Of course we weren't foolish enough to jump our horses over barbed-wire fences, but where we found breaks in the wire, we trespassed, possessed by a pioneer's sense of entitlement.

The terrain that we crossed on horseback seemed as varied as continents, and we named each parcel for its distinctive traits, like explorers would have done. We called a sun-blasted barren field "Wester." A lush acreage bordered by tall black cedars that floated above the land like unbottled genies we named "Greenfields" after a popular wistful song by the Kingston Trio. The fact that we were smitten by the nearly holy loveliness of these places—so much so that we were compelled to lavish lyrical titles upon them—suggests to me that at twelve or thirteen we not only cherished but feared losing them. Naming the fields and woods that we traversed gave them permanence. How could a young, reckless girl, cometing her horse across a meadow, foresee the end of such completely healthy wildness, bring her horse to a halt, and for an instant grieve for the delicacy of her joy and what might become of it? But I say that more than once, this happened to us. We were nostalgic for our girlhoods even before we began to lose them. It was 1960. Ours may have been the last uncynical girlhoods possible in America.

We took risks, imperiled ourselves in a thousand ways, might have killed ourselves a time or two but for luck or good timing. Daring had nothing to do with our boldness; freedom did. We ordered and dispensed all our own grain and hay; we phoned the vets and farriers. Sometimes the horses broke out of their fences and we chased them down Westridge Road, stopping traffic, racing through people's yards, ducking clotheslines, sweet-talking to lure them back. Once, in a runaway, somebody was nearly beheaded when her horse dashed under the grape arbor. Once we found newborn kittens who had been cannibalized by wasps. At the barn we entered a world more harrowing and unsparing in its lessons in brutality and coarseness than our parents ever suspected. We saturated ourselves with it, yielded entirely to its roughness, its flashes of grace.

On school mornings, when it was my turn to feed, my father drove me to the barn. I remember entering the feed room in my pristine school clothes, sensing the barn's trove of squalor and longing to stay. I felt like an imposter in the clothes. I imagined the horses would laugh jeerfully when they saw me. My father waited patiently in the warm car, listening to Bob Poole's radio show, while I vanished into a dusk of odor and chore, smashing skins of ice off the water troughs with my bare hands, marveling at the freeze-swollen hoofprints in the muddy corral. Early sun hazed through dusty panes in the hayloft windows, and the room gleamed like a vault stacked with gold, not straw. Downstairs, snug in their stalls, our horses stomped and nickered. As they chewed the oats and corn that I'd poured into their bins, the crunch of their big jaws made me swallow with longing, made me sniff deeply, nose-wallowingly for the steam-grainy scent of their breaths pluming brownly into the cold air. I wanted to eat my own cereal that loud.

At school, I felt like the Clark Kent version of my Superman self. My hands looked awkward in repose, scratched and bruised, the insides of my palms and fingers waxy-tough from tugging off baling wire and jerking reins. I clunked around, tall, gawky, and flat-chested. I wore powder-blue harlequin glasses and big fat biscuit-looking tie-shoes for arch support because I had pronated ankles. Everybody else scooted around the hallways in slim loafers. On rare occasion I was invited to a make-out party by some loser boy who had mysteriously deemed me worth a try; but I was not interested in making out. I seemed to be permanently encased in a protective aura of Barnness. If there had been a boy who looked like Cherokee, I might have been tempted. Young teenage boys are only physically dissimilar from horses: they are human versions, behaving with the same plodding indifference and erratic civility toward a young girl's worshipfulness.

I turned thirteen, fourteen; I entered eighth grade. Some afternoons, after school, I rode a different bus—not home, but to the barn. I didn't know many of the kids I sat with. One cocky, older high school boy named Kenny rode the Westridge Road bus, and he began to pay attention to me. His stop was farther down the road, but he frequently threatened to disembark at mine and follow me up to the barn. He had a lank flag of oaky blonde hair and wet, pouty rock-singer lips. He wore dark glasses, but whenever he slid them down the bridge of his nose to peer more closely at me I saw that his eyes were the icy blue of breath mints. He carried a rabbit's foot on a chain for good luck, and he was always taking it out and trying to swing it in front of some girl's face to hypnotize her.

"Where's it at?" he said, craning his neck to try to see the barn through the trees. "I don't see no barn."

"It's way back behind Mr. Lambeth's house. You can't see it from the road," I told him, hastily gathering up my books.

"Is there a hayloft? I sure do love a hayloft."

"It's private property," I told him sternly. His lackeys, toad-shaped younger boys, would laugh.

"I want to see the hayloft, Blondie."

"I already told you it's private property, no boys allowed."

"Well, maybe I forgot you told me that," Kenny said, grinning. "Or maybe I just happened to be out for a walk one day and got lost and accidentally wandered into the private property that I forgot you told me about. Next I found the hayloft and you were up inside it. What would you do then?"

I couldn't judge his intentions or the narrow distance between flirtation and meanness. I didn't know what I would do if he surprised me in the hayloft. I only hoped he was teasing.

"I'd scream if I was her," said one of the toad boys, and everybody laughed, including me. "Hey, Blondie!" they shouted out the bus windows as I scurried off the bus and down Mr. Lambeth's driveway. "Invite Kenny to go riding with you some day. Hey, girl!"

By twilight on such an afternoon, if I were the only girl up at the barn, if I were scooping out feed, every muted creak, as the barn shifted and settled in the evening cool, every wind-jittered pane spooked me. I jumped if a horse snorted or pawed. I imagined Kenny's loose, oily shadow spilling down the stairs from the loft into the feed and tack room where I worked, and my heart pounded with the dread of reckoning.

He never came, but I listened for him, and I tried to determine what I would say when he finally detached himself from the shadows. If by his teasing he had diminished the haven I'd always believed the barn provided, then I owed him anger. Yet a part of me was made restive by his threats of invasion, tantalized. I even thought I understood his bluster. It was similar to our charging our horses at fences too high to jump or entering brooding posted land, snarly with vines, daring something perilous, pushing beyond our means of easy gain.

I began to think of Kenny when I brushed and curried Cherokee. I had too much time to think. I imagined him slipping up on me and fastening his hand over my mouth like a gag. I imagined myself screaming. But Sunny and I were always screaming and laughing and hollering over something, and who might distinguish one sort of scream from another? I imagined myself going limp, perhaps fainting, and Kenny leading or carrying me into the loft and kissing me there. I imagined that his lips would be warm and soft, not brutal. I imagined Mr. Lambeth, who couldn't hear the scream, hearing the kiss and rushing up to the barn, bursting in on us, furious at my betrayal, and how shabby I would feel for breaking the long-held taboo, NO BOYS ALLOWED. I pictured my unstoppable leakage of tears as I tried to explain myself, knowing full well that what I had done was irrevocable. Whatever was happening to me felt dire and skulking, panicky and profuse.

In the months that followed, I was not unhappy, not bored. I felt vaguely uneasy, as if I had mislaid something vital. The barn felt vacuous, my chores mechanical. The windows at sundown flashed unbearably luminous; the moon seemed too full and Cherokee too simple. I could not stop thinking about the benefits of being elsewhere. Was it boys I gave up my girlhood for—or was it ambition? Was it mistaking one for the other? Soon I would sell Cherokee to a cowboy who wanted to show him Western Pleasure. I had misgivings. To an English rider like myself, the thought of dressing a horse in the heavy, ornate gear of western tack seemed the clodhopper equivalent of outfitting him for the Grand Ole Opry. I felt as if I were selling Cherokee to a foreign country, betraying our manners and style, but on the day the man led him away my heart didn't lurch. He was, after all, just a horse.

In time, my father bought me a thoroughbred hunter named Golden Wonder who we hauled to horse shows in a trailer painted gold, hitched to my mother's Golden Anniversary series Chevrolet Super-Sport. For Christmas, just before my fifteenth birthday, I requested a fancy new saddle, which my parents ordered through Bocock-Stroud in Winston-Salem. The saddle, imported from England and shipped rolled up in a barrel, was the dry golden color of cured tobacco. It was too big for me. I sloshed around in it. No matter how much I soaped and oiled it, I could not subdue the saddle's upstart color; I could not make the leather look tried and true.

I don't know what became of the antique cavalry saddle that I had used with Cherokee. I remember only that I ditched it, that it seemed a clod of leather when compared with its English replacement.

"I'll bet it was valuable," my new friend Stinky Russell said. "I'll bet it was a relic from some historic battle, maybe the Battle of the Little Bighorn."

We were saddling our horses to go foxhunting with the Sedgefield Hunt Club. Stinky was a short, squat boy with blunt, somnolent features and a ragged haircut. When he put on his black velvet helmet and pulled it down low over his eyes, he looked princely. I had a crush on him. I'd never known a boy who could ride better than me. He rode a tall black spirited horse named Curfew, and his father served as master of the hounds. Boys and men were not only allowed to join the hunt club, they ruled it.

"Big mistake to junk a saddle like that," Stinky chided, swinging aboard Curfew in his confident, athletic way. He looked disappointed as he trotted off, and I urged Golden Wonder after him, compelled, I guess, to admit to him my hastiness and vanity in tossing out the old cavalry saddle. What made me want to apologize? What had I been thinking of when I threw the old saddle away, other than riding my new horse in style?

We began to gallop side by side and were nearly airborne with speed before I realized my danger. I could not rein my horse in. I'd meant only to keep abreast of my friend, but passing him, I leaned into a wind as full of thrash and undertow as riptide. My horse streaked past the huntmaster in his scarlet coat, his horn bleating not merely the news of my transgression against hunt protocol but my imminent dissoluteness.

The author and her father, Roderick Mark
Buie Jr., on Guam, where she was born
while he was stationed there in the navy.

The author and her mother, Betty Jane Buie, at the
beach, 1952.

The author with brother "Knothead" at the Starmount
Forest house, 1954.

Mother and the family's new 1956 Buick.

The family dressed for church, ca. 1956.

The house in Starmount Forest, 1954.

The "heartfelt home" in Sunset Hills.

The time of horses: Sunny (left) with Queen, author with Cherokee and Knothead.

The author at sixteen with Golden Wonder—Goldy for short.

The author with sons Sam and Roderick; marquee in background promotes her book-signing.

The Rodeo Parade

SUNNY AND I were thirteen that summer and brave about most everything except the wasps that lived in the hayloft. The sound we heard coming from the loft one morning was a high-pitched hum, sinuous, like the whine of a distant drill, and we suspected the wasps, imagined them sharpening their stingers, plotting some terrorist deed. I climbed the stairs to investigate, ducking to avoid any crossfire.

I didn't like crawling into the loft in summer. Its windows faced south, the sashes so swollen that the glass could only be raised a couple of inches. The air smelled molten. All day long sunlight banged into the room like solid sheets of tin roofing and wasps and mud daubers tasseled the heated air. Their fluted nests and slapdash adobes barnacled the rafters.

I wasn't afraid of the mud daubers, who avoided confrontation and kept busy with their secretive insect projects. The wasps, however, were bullies. I crouched warily beneath their ominous drift. They flew stupidly, without a clear mission, dragging their legs through the air in deranged and thuggish ballet. What was their purpose in life? To hector and antagonize.

At the top of the stairs, I saw at once what was making the sound. Tucked into a pocket of hay, where they had most likely been born a day or two earlier, lay three feeble kittens. I shouted excitedly down to Sunny, guessing that the wild pregnant cat we'd seen slinking around the barn had birthed her kittens there. But by the time Sunny had raced upstairs to join me, I'd stooped to take a closer look, and my view had turned ghastly. Although alive enough to peep their agony, the kittens bristled with wasps. Their eyes had been partially eaten out and their bodies were tumored by stings. It wasn't the kittens who writhed in their nest, but the insects and maggots who feasted upon them.

We rolled the kittens onto a feed sack and carried them, as if by tiny stretcher, downstairs, away from the heat and bombardment. We dippered cool water over their wounds and scraped off maggots with sticks. In spite of our ministrations, we suspected the kittens could not be saved. We allowed that they would *rather* be dead. As children, we were on the wavelength of most animals; we tried to speak for them. Because the feral kittens were unfamiliar to us—not like pets—we could be stoic. In their blind, pathetic meekness they suffered. In our hands they weighed less than leaves.

We expected the poor creatures to wind down as we watched, but instead they torqued and strained and cawed into the void that was their meager life. We had not expected death to look so labored. As children we were not yet aware that life is something every creature fights mightily toward, not against, and that dying is rarely peaceful or easy or dignified or without the frenzy of clawing after life no matter how ragged life's edges.

We didn't know how to kill them, but since we concurred that they were better off dead, we felt obliged to find the best way to carry out the sentence. We were serious about our enterprise, strangely more charged with determination than sorrow. We had something to prove to ourselves, I think. The word maturity comes to mind, but it is still a dreadful word to me: unctuous, suggestive of past-ripened hormones and platitudes.

We considered drowning them, and I can't remember why we didn't.

We considered stomping them flat with our boots, burying them alive.

We began to wish we'd never found the blighted things. The Collins family lived next door to Mr. Lambeth; their backyard adjoined our barnyard. When I heard Mr. Collins's car putter into his driveway, I had a brainstorm: we'd put the kittens into a sack and attach the sack to the tailpipe of the car. Hadn't we learned in science that car exhaust—carbon monoxide—was a deadly gas? In elementary school, we'd traveled to Raleigh to visit both the North Carolina Art Museum and the State Penitentiary. At the penitentiary we'd toured the electric chair and the gas chamber. We kids had all agreed that the gas chamber looked more humane. It was a simple little room with a cot. The gas was dispensed through a vent in the ceiling. A friendly official assured us that lethal gas smelled as pleasant as peach blossoms.

And so Sunny and I chose the gas chamber for the kittens who were innocent of any crime. I suppose we felt less guilty about our decision after Mr. Collins examined them and agreed with us that their lives weren't salvageable. We deposited them, one by tiny one, into a thick paper grocery bag, then tied the bag onto the end of the car's exhaust pipe with baling twine. We wore gardening gloves to protect our hands while Mr. Collins revved the engine and we readjusted the drooping sack. It took a long time for the kittens to die. We kept untying and squinting into the bag, to determine if we'd gassed them long enough.

After we buried them and marked their graves with little twig crosses, we lost our spirit for riding that day. We felt dismayed and confused by our courage, our devotion to such a strict mission. Grazing in the pasture, our horses gleamed conceitedly, like trophies. They buried their muzzles in the bountiful grass swishing their sashy tails. They took their strength for granted and were no more grateful for their health and good fortune than hulking, glossy furniture (or despots). That they shrugged off the sting of an insect with an involuntary rippling of muscle conveyed to us a runaway injustice in the world.

We didn't dwell on the death of the kittens for long, but our consensual responsibility for their executions, the load of tenderhearted bewilderment that followed, forged a bond between Sunny and me. We felt both wise among our friends and conspiratorially ugly. Sometimes I suspected that we'd killed the kittens not out of mercy but because we were curious about death, ignorant of its machinery and wanting to see it ticking up close.

❧

That fall a traveling rodeo came to town, preceded by much advertising fanfare and an invitation, printed in local newspapers, for residents to participate in a downtown parade. Sunny and I immediately signed up and informed our parents.

"How do you plan to get that stubborn mule of yours downtown?" my father asked, recalling Cherokee's staunch reluctance to load onto a van.

"We're going to *ride* downtown."

"But it's too far," my mother protested. "I'll bet it's a six-mile ride from the barn. When is the parade?"

"A week from Friday."

"On a school day?"

Later, when I overheard my mother discussing our plans with Sunny's mom, I could tell by her genial laughter that our parents were going to say yes. They were pleased that our enthusiasm for plotting tomboyish excursions had not diminished. We weren't a bit like some of the girls our age who wore make-up to school and peroxided their hair and made out on the school bus with steamy abandon.

Our biggest hurdle, then, was in finding a way to look authentically western. To assume convincing roles as rodeo gals, we needed proper cowgirl attire and big glitzy western saddles. Between us, we owned a hodgepodge of hand-me-down English tack.

One afternoon, shuffling around Friendly Shopping Center buying school supplies, we halted in front of Belk's department store, agog. It was as if we'd daydreamed the window display into existence.

Amid a pyramid of hay bales, two girlish mannequins sporting gold
and silver lamé cowgirl suits, their arms linked do-si-do style, smiled
glassily down at us. What frozen fun they seemed to be having.
In front of them, astride sawhorses, sat two kingly western saddles,
one studded with silver and the other with gold. We observed that the
mannequins looked like us. "Dibs on the silver one," Sunny said.
"Dibs on the gold," said I. We hurried into the store and asked a clerk
if the costumes were for sale. She didn't think they were and referred
us to Mr. Cocklereece, the manager.

Mr. Cocklereece received us into his flourescent-lit office with a
formal handshake, but his scrutinizing gaze made me feel like a
shoplifter. He patiently explained to us that the gold and silver costumes were not for sale. "They're on loan from Blue Bell Manufacturing," he said. "The company is sponsoring the rodeo that's coming
to town, and our display is part of the promotion. Do you girls know
about the rodeo?"

"Do we know about the rodeo!" we smirked.

"You don't suppose that we could *borrow* the outfits, do you?"
Sunny asked. Before he could object, she launched into a spiel of self-
promotion. We'd only need the costumes for one day; we'd treat them
with respect and return them in immaculate condition; our parents
would agree to a damage deposit; it would be excellent public relations for the store; we'd never shop any department store but Belk's
from that day forward—even though they did not carry Villager
brand dresses.

When Sunny had finished making her pitch, Mr. Cocklereece stood
up to dismiss us. "I'm sorry, girls," he said flatly, "but the costumes
aren't mine to loan."

Outside Belk's, waiting for Sunny's mother to pick us up, we paced
and groused. "Why so pouty?" Mrs. Oliver asked as we slid into the
backseat.

She seemed amused by our account of meeting with Mr. Cocklereece. She laughed, not at our efforts to connive the costumes away
from him, but at his effort to hold on to them. I'd never seen an adult
so readily disregard the judgment of one of their kind. Mostly adults

belonged to one staunch, pragmatic club and we children belonged to some loosey-goosey other. Halfway to my house, Mrs. Oliver suddenly veered into somebody's driveway and reversed direction.

"Where are we going, Mom?" Sunny asked.

"I believe I need to speak with Mr. Cocklereece myself," her mother said. Streaming through the rolled-down car windows, the wind puffed up her hair like a warrior's headdress.

I didn't know Mrs. Oliver very well. My friendship with her daughter had developed over the months that Sunny and I had spent at Mr. Lambeth's barn. We did not hang out at one another's houses. I didn't even know if Mrs. Oliver was the sort of mother who baked cookies. I considered her lively and attentive, less gushy than my own mother perhaps, but not dulled by housewifery as some of my mother's friends seemed to be. She was small-boned, graceful, trim, with dark brown feathery hair cropped short and a heart-shaped face like her beautiful daughter, Helen, Sunny's older sister. I had the impression that Mrs. Oliver read a lot and played tennis. I considered her more serene than expressive, which is why I was surprised when she turned her car around and headed impulsively into the fray of Mr. Cocklereece. She looked like she was hungry for a fight.

We didn't go into Belk's with her. I felt nervous for her, as if we'd sent her off on an impractical, even dangerous, dare. I knew that my own mother would not have confronted Mr. Cocklereece on our behalf. I suspected that she would have thought our begging to borrow the costumes unmannerly and presumptuous.

When she returned to the car, Mrs. Oliver was beaming. "You've got your costumes, girls," she said. "You've got the saddles, too."

"The saddles! How did you do it?" we squealed. "What did you say?"

My passion for melodrama led me to hope that she'd punched Mr. Cocklereece in the face and bullied the permission out of him. Or that she'd applied her seductive feminine wiles.

"I used pure logic," Mrs. Oliver said brightly. "I simply asked him to call Blue Bell Manufacturing Company and speak to the big cheese who could give permission. You've always got to speak to the big cheese, girls. Remember that."

"And he did it? He called?"

"What else could the man do? His only excuse for not lending the costumes was that some big cheese might object."

We giggled and she giggled, and we stopped at the Guilford Dairy Bar for ice cream cones to celebrate, even though it was nearly suppertime. We clicked our cones together, toasting our good fortune. We were not bratty or vainglorious girls, as Mr. Cocklereece might have thought; we were celebrants at the jubilee of life, and our parents stuck by us, even goaded us toward our pursuits. They didn't just love and champion us, they approved of us to the extent that our dreams ripely felt like an extension of their own.

If I had known what was going to happen in a few months that would change all of us forever, I would have nudged Sunny to notice her mother's smiling profile, to memorize it—the radiance of a winner—and to remember that moment of exultation for as long as she lived, for that moment was at once as gorgeous and uncomplicated as life ever is. There we sat, lapping up our ice cream on an Indian-summer evening, riding home wallowing in a breeze as warm as bath water. In the back seat, Sunny and I kicked off our shoes and stuck bare feet out the windows, wiggling them like victory flags. I imagined Mr. Cocklereece, back at Belk's, tromping around in his hard black airless shoes, performing duties and chores. I suspected that at one time he'd been the sort of dull, worried boy who, had he glanced out a school window one autumn afternoon and seen two young girls trotting down the road on horseback, would have not only lacked the spunk to feel jealous but maligned them as truants.

We spent days grooming our horses for the parade. We curried and brushed them to a watery sheen. Their hides seemed to spark and liquefy beneath the friction of our labor. We trimmed their fetlocks and painted their hooves with black shoe polish and buffed over the polish with wax. We fed them apples and carrots to sweeten their dispositions, and we told them where we planned to take them and lectured them on how they were to behave.

On the morning of the parade, Mrs. Oliver picked up the costumes at Belk's, and we all met at the barn to dress. My golden suit was two sizes too large and hung droopily. My mother cinched the waist and shortened the cuffs with safety pins, little gold ones that blended with the fabric. She was a whiz with safety pins and could position them so that they were completely invisible. This is an art. Mrs. Oliver, who had brought silver safety pins to match Sunny's fabric, performed similar alterations. Did we thank them for their help? I doubt it. We were too excited to feel grateful. Surely they knew, without our saying so, how much we depended upon a mother's fingers, improving, smoothing, tucking in and taking care.

It was a crisp and windy October morning, and we straddled the ornate thrones of our borrowed saddles in our hard-won regalia, shivering. The metallic fabric felt itchy and chilly, as ventilated as window screen. "You girls need your sweaters," my mother cautioned.

We protested. Heck no. Who'd ever seen Dale Evans galloping across the prairie in a skinny-armed pastel nylon cardigan sweater? We gritted our teeth against the cold and took off for downtown.

As we rode past Kiser Junior High School, our alma mater, I nudged Cherokee into a jaunty gait that felt as much like a swagger as cantering. We shouted at the windows where the classrooms were, but nobody looked out. We trotted around the reservoir at Lake Daniel Park, past Edmunds Manufacturing Company and the high-voltage terminals that strutted along Buffalo Creek, past the railroad tracks at the bottom of Hill Street Cemetery, then the cemetery itself. We paused at every intersection, just like cars, for stoplights to flash green. People stared and smiled and waved. We waved back like celebrities.

Downtown in Fisher Park, under a bronzing overhang of oak trees near the First Presbyterian Church, we waited for the parade to begin. Rough-looking, hatless, unshaven men, riding plain brown mud-spattered horses, slouched in their saddles and smoked cigarettes. One of the desperadoes sported loafers, no boots. A column of little girls decked out in red-sequined leotards and white tasseled boots slung batons into the air.

Our parents brought us sandwiches and soft drinks, then they slipped into the crowd of spectators lining up along the curbs. Finally some signal was given. The twirlers lowered their batons and turned poker-faced attention to their leader, who clamped a whistle between her teeth. They were, all of them, fat little show-off girls, as barrel-chested and thin-legged and hoppy as robins.

As the crowd burst into applause, we proceeded up Greene Street, and for a brief, glittering instant I convinced myself that we were rodeo swells, riding as sidekicks: the Silverado Kid and her pal, the Gold Rush Gal. "Say cheese," Mrs. Oliver called and darted out into the street to snap our pictures. The wind whooped and twisted among the canyons of tall buildings. Trash cartwheeled like tumbleweed across the street, spooking our horses. The sunlight was intense, but the shadows more so. My hat blew off, and once I'd retrieved it, I rode the rest of the way encumbered, holding the hat on my head with one hand. The parade was over in five blocks.

"It was fun, wasn't it?" we said.

"It was the best," we said, turning our horses around for the long trip home, riding off into the sunset. Our shadows flickering in the weeds looked gooney.

Back at the barn, we stripped off our costumes, folded them neatly, zippered them into protective plastic bags. "Guess who I ran into at the parade?" Mrs. Oliver said. "Mr. Cocklereece, and he was just as pleasant as could be."

The school year passed uneventfully, the rodeo parade its highlight—that and, perhaps, the opening of the first McDonald's restaurant in Greensboro, located on Summit Avenue. Mrs. Oliver introduced us to McDonald's. She invited my mother and me to join Sunny and her there for lunch. We all enjoyed the food, marveling at its tastiness, but the mothers praised its convenience and cheapness as well. Imagine 15¢ hamburgers and 11¢ bags of French fries speedily prepared! This was revolutionary, liberating food. OVER THREE MILLION SOLD, the sign

beneath the golden arches proclaimed. "Three million already?" my
mother exclaimed. "Where have I been?" She and Mrs. Oliver
laughed the conspiratorial laughter of busy mothers on the go, always
looking for ways to lighten their domestic loads without shortchang-
ing their families. They looked young in their shirtwaist dresses, bit-
ing into their McDonald's hamburgers. They had tiny waists and
shapely legs and spirited senses of humor.

Soon it was summer again, and the wasps commenced their sentinel drifting in the barn loft. We were not as afraid of them as before.
The wild cat who had birthed her litter the year before did not return.
It was a soft and dreamy time, stretching before us, wide open and
fruitful, the Great Plains of childhood.

Lush swags of honeysuckle and trumpet vine sagged upon our
fences. The pasture grass grew tall and thick, inky green with
whirlpools of shade into which the horses seemed to disappear as if
slowly sucked down drains. We carried buckets of feed out to them
where they grazed, but, sated on grass, they were wise to our lures
and evasive. We talked lazily about riding downtown to the Fourth
of July parade, but the weather was too hot for scheming. The cut
fields looked as brown and scabby as the scorched tops of ironing
boards. When we rode, we strolled the horses through cool woodland
trails we knew about that dead-ended in orchards or meadows sudsy
with Queen Anne's lace, flowers so beautiful that you forgot they were
filled with mites and chiggers.

One morning my mother, who was not in the habit of waking me
because we had no schedule to keep, touched my shoulder. I yawned,
stretched luxuriously, inhaling the pungent green motory fragrance
of a lawnmower toiling in some neighbor's yard, feeling prodigal with
languor, coins of sunlight scattering easy-come, easy-go across my
sheet. "Wake up, honey," my mother said. "I've got some bad news."
I bolted upright, and when she was certain I was clear-headed, she
took my hand and said, "Mrs. Oliver was killed in a car wreck last
night."

I could hear my father pacing around downstairs. It was nearly
nine o'clock. Normally he would have been making his rounds at the

hospital. I suppose he was reluctant to leave for work until he'd seen me through the initial trauma of such a horrendous piece of news. I could not absorb it. "*Sunny's* mother?" I kept saying over and over. "Sunny's *mother?*"

I pictured her rushing out of Belk's, her face flushed with excitement and bravado as she told us how she'd vanquished Mr. Cocklereece. I saw her squinting into her camera, framing us for posterity as we paraded forth in our rodeo costumes. I remembered the appreciative way she'd lifted the bun off her McDonald's burger to admire its fragrant contents. Nobody's mother got killed in car wrecks, nobody's mother whom you knew and liked and had ridden happily beside in the very car that she had crashed. It sounded cheap and overwrought.

The Taylor family lived across the street from us. Mrs. Taylor was my Girl Scout leader, and her daughter, Jill, was good friends with both Sunny and me. Earlier Mrs. Taylor had phoned my parents and notified them about the accident. Sunny was coming to spend the day with Jill while Mr. Oliver made funeral arrangements. Mrs. Taylor had invited me to join them and had told my parents that Jill was counting on my company.

I dressed and ate breakfast, but I dawdled. I tried to force myself to cry, but I couldn't squeeze forth a single tear. I suspected the tears were building within me and would release of their own accord; but I wanted to get them over with. I didn't want the surprise of them in front of Sunny. Truthfully, I was in no hurry to see her. I was accustomed to her crusty, tomboyish poise; I'd never seen her cry—even when she fell off a horse once and loosened her front tooth. She never panicked, never yelped. She was level-headed, unflappable. I imagined how I would behave if my own mother had died the night before in a car wreck. They would have dragged me screaming and kicking from my house to sit with Jill Taylor all day. I would have fallen into a coma of grief, locked myself in a darkened bedroom and cried myself to death by dehydration. How could Sunny show up at Jill's house and do anything but sob into her hands all day? I dreaded witnessing her pain; it seemed the worst violation of someone's privacy. I was afraid of her, of what she had become overnight—a mourner—when before she'd been my sidekick in celebration. I knew that when I saw her, my instinct would be to hug her although I had never hugged her before. I had enormous heart for her troubles, but my heart felt all thumbs.

She appeared at the Taylor's house, calm and dry-eyed. I'd expected a grim dishevelment—the demeanor of an orphan—but her hair was neatly combed and she wasn't dressed in black. When I embraced her, she felt as unyielding as a broomstick.

"We're so sorry," Jill said with eager kindness, and Sunny shrugged, looking almost apologetic. I'd expected a faded version of her, but there she stood, her same tanned rough-hewn self, wearing shorts and sandals. Her calmness convinced us that she was glad to be among friends, a good sport about her loss, a charming diplomat for death. She had appetite for both lunch and games. We played endless rounds of jacks and Chinese checkers. We played the card game Oh Hell. We delighted in slapping our cards down and shouting "Oh hell!" within earshot of Mrs. Taylor, but she never reprimanded us. We listened to rock and roll on WCOG. We whiled away the afternoon on the Taylors' screened porch, drinking iced tea, smelling the steamy weather, the pine mulch baking, listening to a woodpecker's insistent nattering on a nearby tree, observing the lolling radiance of sun-filled leaves overhead, a soaring blue sky streaky with the exhaust trails of jets. We talked all around the sinkhole of Mrs. Oliver's death, nearly talking ourselves out of it. A ladybug alighted on my shoulder—always a sign of good luck. "Ladybug, ladybug, fly away home, your house is on fire and your children will burn." I wished I hadn't said it.

Close to five, the paperboy heaved a *Greensboro Record* up the Taylor's driveway, but none of us moved to retrieve it. The sorrowful news inside the paper lay ticking like a bomb. Across the street was the reassuring sight of my mother's Plymouth station wagon parked in our drive. My mother, safe at home, was probably baking a pie to cheer me up. I envisioned her standing at the kitchen sink, gazing in our direction, feeling sorry for us all, the strain we now labored under to be girls together, just *girls*. I hoped that she wouldn't come outside and walk across the street and make some gesture of condolence. Just the thought of her gathering Sunny into her arms, the sweet almond fragrance of the Jergens hand lotion she always wore, made my heart fragile with the sense that I had gone too long without telling her that I loved her. I didn't want Sunny to see her or to notice her Plymouth parked loyally in front of our house, reminding her that everybody else's mothers were steadfastly alive and cooking supper for their children in spite of her loss. It was a worrisome revelation to me: that the world hardly paused for death, that my mother and Mrs. Taylor kept diligently at their daily tasks and chores. Nobody fell into a heap, protesting the fate of the fallen mother. I thought all of us ought to have gone a little mad for a while, but instead we pretended to an order and stability that either did not exist, apart from our vigilant insistence, or was, at best, temporary.

Wiping her hands on the hem of her apron, Mrs. Taylor walked outside to collect the newspaper. She unfolded it, scanned the front page, then strolled up the driveway to where we all bunched on the screen porch stoop. She handed Sunny the paper, and I caught a glimpse on the front page photo of dead, vivacious Mrs. Oliver. "You'll want to read the article, honey," she told Sunny.

"Not now." Sunny set the paper aside. "I already know what happened."

"Do you want to talk about it?" Mrs. Taylor suggested softly.

"No."

"We know you're still in shock," Jill said.

Sunny shrugged. "I've already talked about it with Dad and Helen. All last night. Dad came straight home from the hospital and told us everything."

It was a relief to finally talk about the accident, and the relief made me giddy. "I'll bet you stayed up all night. How could you sleep? I sure couldn't have," I said almost cheerfully.

"We just lay down in one big clump," Sunny said. "We talked and hugged and cried all night."

"In the same bed?" I asked.

She nodded.

"Gosh," I said. "Weird," I said, and perhaps I even looked appalled. "With your *father?*"

What did I mean? I was trying to make digressive conversation, still trying to avert a head-on collision with death. I'd said what I'd said in a subversive, silly attempt to normalize our conversation, to bring it within range of topics that might inspire familiar reactions or agreement. Under normal conditions, teenagers did not share beds with their parents. But no matter how I attempted to justify the remark, I knew that it had been a terrible breach of kindness, of tact. I had implied that to be motherless was so strange a predicament that one was bound to behave perversely. I had suggested that from this day forward Sunny would be considered half-orphaned, and all sorts of make-do arrangements—from sleeping in the same bed with distraught relatives to eating TV dinners because none of the survivors knew how to cook—would complicate her life. She gazed upon me as if I were a speck in the distance, as if she couldn't quite distinguish who I was, then she put her face into her hands and began to sob.

Over the years I would hear rumors that, prior to the accident, Mrs. Oliver had been drinking. She had met her husband at a party, but why were they traveling separately? Perhaps Mr. Oliver had run late at the office and phoned her to meet him there. Maybe it was a party one of them had forgotten about or hadn't wanted to attend. I liked to think that Mrs. Oliver had planned to stay home that evening with her daughters, had felt annoyed when her husband called her late from work to remind her about the party. Maybe she'd felt rushed, couldn't find the right dress to wear, needed to wash her hair. By all accounts, it seemed that she was not where she wanted to be that night. Maybe Mr. Oliver got angry with her for dancing with another man that night. I have always pictured lovely Mrs. Oliver swirling across the dance floor, only minutes from her death, dancing cheek-to-cheek with some big cheese. Whatever the catalyst, it was rumored that she and Mr. Oliver argued. She left the party hastily and he followed her in a separate car. In trying to outdistance him, she misjudged a vicious curve on Cornwallis Drive and plowed into a telephone pole.

Was it possible that Sunny finally burst into tears because her father, lying that sad night in bed with his two daughters, had whispered a similar innocence-wrecking story too bleak to share with us? Perhaps my remark undid her in some uncanny way, reminding her of how she'd come to know such bitter facts and from whom.

I placed a hand on her trembling shoulder.

"It's all right," Mrs. Taylor told me, "let her have a good cry."

Touching her, I detected the superheated engine of her misery. Her humid skin felt contagious with grief, and I began to cry, too. Young and inexperienced, I was probably crying mostly for myself, not for Sunny, not for her dead mother. I was crying for my shameful awkwardness, the inept solace I'd offered and bungled, for life's divisive labyrinths that lead us to momentous brinks where some jump off and some do not and an unlucky few are pushed. One grief connected to another grief as if by links of chain. I cried for the dissipating glory of all our past parades, for an extravagant innocence gone begging. I could hear us brashly ordering our mothers *please* not to insist that we wear those insipid sweaters over our costumes, *please* to let us make our own choices and live with them, suffer the consequences, *please* not to treat us like babies. But we were babies, and why be ashamed? We were hardly more capable of saving ourselves than the kittens we'd found in the loft. With all my heart I wished that we could go back and make amends with the innocence we'd spurned, all the way back to the day we'd found the kittens, only this time we would work diligently to save them.

What I had not learned yet but now believe is that the demise of innocence is piecemeal and rarely completed during the course of one's long life, that innocence—both gift and imposition—is infinitely regenerative. The only way we are ever shaken loose from it is over and over and over again.

"Here," Sunny said, passing me a Kleenex, "what are you crying so hard for?"

I could not bear to collaborate with sorrow. We were so small and underfoot and death was a brutal giant pounding down. I only knew about those things that were alive and good. I could not stop exulting in our faintest remnants, clinging to Mrs. Oliver by those precious gold and silver threads. They were out there somewhere, still floating in the lustrous wind, tangible little anchors to a parade gone past.

I didn't say a word, not one of comfort or of fear. I put my arms around my friend and we could feel each other holding on for dearest life.

Becky's Accident

AT THE BARN we knew what we were doing by instinct, enchantment, intuition—all those instant puddings of reason. We knew by pressing our foreheads to the lovely starred brows of our horses and telepathing their designs. You could hear the thunder of our colliding brainstorms. Our tenacity and gall was matched only by the horsefly's.

In return for our discipleship, the horses agreed to serve as guides and interpreters, to decode and alert us to all treacheries that lurked in the fields and woods that we traveled. They knew best those phenomena which sought to unseat us: mole holes in tall grass, the swat of low branches, hornet nests, the menacing signature a copperhead scrawled across a trail, barbed wire materializing suddenly like air basted with darts. In return for the jitter of us that enlivened their grazed-calm minds and kept their placid stares from becoming as muddy-dumb as the gaze of cows, they permitted us to posture upon their backs, not as equals or bosses, but more like muses, thinking up things for them to do. We mistook our inventiveness for power, resting atop them in a catatonia of ease, as trusting as if we'd sunk ourselves in lounge chairs.

We muses knew what we were doing, tumbling like stunt men from the hayloft to land astride our horses bareback, riding them without bridles, steering them with wispy bits of baling string looped around their necks. We made them take vows: no shying, no rolling in mud after we'd curried and brushed their hides until their rumps gleamed like caramel apples, no breaking wind in public, no runaways. We galloped them into deep, uncharted lakes. Our skins pressed against them, reading the large heaving Braille of their musculature, and we believed that they would never turn against us, that our partnership softened them; our kisses turned them stupid. I'd taught my heavy, lazy plowhorse, Cherokee, how to jump. Nobody could tell me that he hadn't learned to do it out of love.

Before I owned Cherokee, I often begged my mother to drive me twelve miles into the country to Sedgefield Stables on the Groomtown Road, where for two dollars an hour I could rent a horse and plod around a ring. I fought for her to take me against the riptide demands of my brothers. I'm sure that more than once I peeled her away from some heart's desire of her own. I'd find her sitting cross-legged on the living room floor with her art supplies set out: the wooden box of pastels, drawing pencils, art gum erasers, the photographs of us children as babies that she intended to copy. She hunched doggedly over her work, as vulnerable as a covered wagon, while around her whooped my renegade brothers. There was little peace to be had in our house during daylight: the bamming of screen doors sounded like frantic Morse code. There was no martyrdom among us children; instead, lots of braying, writhing, and bellowing blame, the veins standing out on our necks as thick as bell pulls while we hollered. She sat in the middle of it, undeterred, patiently trying to make art.

I thought nothing of interrupting her to plead that she drive me to the riding stables. If she mumbled a mild, distracted "no," I badgered. She launched the word with all the confidence of a Captain standing on a sinking ship, a female captain whose motto was Men

and Children First. Any trip out to Sedgefield would inevitably in-
volve her bundling up the baby and taking him along. She'd have to
jolly him for a carbound hour if he wouldn't sleep.

At Sedgefield, they regularly saddled up a horse named Juniper for
me. She was the plainest horse in the stable: a roach-colored, sway-
backed mare with tall floppy mule's ears and light patches of hair surrounding her eyes that reminded me of the goggle-size spectacles Mrs.
Shelburn, our school librarian, wore. Around and around I rode in a
going-nowhere circle on a horse that looked as if she would have been
much happier curled up in her stall reading a good book. Juniper's
pokiness went beyond the docility of a school horse; it was more akin
to depression. I felt depressed riding her: her gait was incorrectably
ratchety, like a shopping cart with one screwball wheel. Her canter
was lumpy, not carbonated, more like a ride over speed bumps. You
couldn't get her to quicken her pace unless you banged her hard in
the ribs with your sharpest heels, and I was at the tender age when I
couldn't bear the cruelty of banging a horse in the ribs. Maybe I had
such an unhappy time riding Juniper because she seemed to be on my
mother's browbeaten wavelength. Beyond the ring, I glimpsed Mother
inside the car, bouncing my fussy brother, playing patty-cake, feeding
him his bottle, running the engine so that she could keep the radio
and heater going for comfort. Sometimes she'd look up and wave at
me, as if I were far away, nearly unrecognizable to her.

I understood the sacrifices my mother made for my well-being and
pleasure, which was one of the reasons I didn't quickly disparage her
opinions when I became a horsier and more strong-willed girl. Most of
the time her assessments made good sense; but her worries over my
safety and her attempts at interference were intolerable when they
pertained to Barn Life. She knew zero about horses, wasn't interested
in knowing, didn't even own a pair of jeans, kept her hands clean, her
fingernails polished, her hair tidy, and always smelled sweet. If she'd
investigated Barn Life for herself, she would have been shocked at our
penchant for filth and risky enterprise. She ascertained only that I was
completely happy spending my time there. What parent questions or
feels urged to pry into a child's clear-eyed ongoing contentment?

Once, at a horse show, when my mount refused a jump and reared up in protest, nearly throwing me off, my mother, horrified, reared up from her seat in the grandstand, too. I glimpsed her big sun hat and the Audrey Hepburn dark glasses. I sensed her ferocious panic charging at me like another hurdle. "GET OFF THAT HORSE!" she shouted. "GET OFF *now!*" I didn't obey. I tried to pretend that she was a lunatic stranger, but my face flamed.

My horse had been wise to refuse the jump. In practice, we'd never taken fences higher than three-and-a-half feet, and going into the ring I'd been cautioned that the jumps were set at four. My horse, a mathematical wizard, had figured the discrepancy, felt betrayed by my risk taking, and decided she'd teach me a lesson. She was the only mother I'd hearken to under those circumstances. Her balking at the jump was her way of punishing me for doing something without her consultation and permission.

"GET OFF THAT DAMN HORSE," my mother shouted. "DO YOU WANT TO GET KILLED?"

Instead, I nudged Goldy toward the four-foot bar so that she could nibble and befriend it and gauge the hurdle better. We backed up, trotted a second warmup circle, and galloped forward. She took the fence faultlessly, and despite her earlier refusal, we won a fourth-place ribbon.

Sometimes I believed I'd come to a point where the contributions my parents had made to my life and the contributions my horses had made were no longer running neck-and-neck. The horses were edging them out.

On school days, my mother usually picked me up at the barn around dusk. My riding buddy Becky, who lived less than a half mile away, rode her bike home. She had to be home promptly at six to help Squeaky the cook prepare dinner. Her father expected the family to assemble and sit down to a meal at 6:30 sharp. They ate in a cavernous dining room under the dazzling stalactites of a crystal chandelier.

Becky lived in a weathered mansion just inside the city limits that had once been the sumptuous residence of the notorious Junius Scales, most famous for his Communist affiliations and activities before and during the McCarthy era. In 1951 he'd been arrested by the FBI for violating the Smith Act and brought to trial for advocating the violent overthrow of the United States government.

Scales was from a prominent Greensboro family, and his trial had scandalized the community. He actually served eighteen months of a six-year prison sentence in the Guilford County jail before President Kennedy granted him clemency. The house of his boyhood bore evidence of a privileged upbringing despite its poor maintenance by later owners.

Exotic painted murals depicting leafy, Gauguin-inspired vistas decorated the foyer walls and hallways. There was a secret panel in the library and a dumb-waiter in the kitchen. The house had nine tiled bathrooms with old porcelain tubs, fixtures, pedestal sinks, high-backed toilets (not all of which functioned), and a stairwell that ascended to a remote third story where there was a ballroom with a bandstand. Becky's eccentric older sister, Tara (who looked like Sylvia Plath), chose to inhabit a lonesome bedroom on the third floor and painted one wall with a life-size tree whose sketchy branches spread across the ceiling and seemed to be menacingly tipped with long, pointed fingernails.

The doors to all the rooms in the house had old-fashioned, ornate keyholes you could easily spy through and that locked with the turn of a skeleton key. There were two enormous kitchens with outdated appliances, light bulbs dangling overhead that operated by pull-chains, scuffed linoleum countertops, sinks with exposed plumbing, a spacious walk-in larder, and, in the laundry room where the maid spent a good deal of her time, a professional mangle for ironing.

This was the house I imagined when I later read *The Turn of the Screw*. Radiators clanked and rumbled, shrieked and huffed. You could lie in bed there and imagine you heard mice skittering along the baseboards in the dark, or Tara's fingernail tree scratching to escape confinement and join the wild surrounding forest, or ghosts drifting and cooing up and down the stairwell, or the sinister creak of a somnambulist's wheelchair. The house faced gloomy, vine-choked woodland and an expanse of lawn that tilted toward Hamilton Lake, where the drowned body of a man wrapped in chains had once been dredged up. This wasn't true, but we sometimes pretended it was. A body had been found in another local lake, wrapped in curtains stolen from a Greensboro motel.

Becky's mother, severely disabled from a stroke she'd suffered years earlier, was wheelchair-bound, but she was not a somnambulist. As a girl, visiting for an overnight, I could hardly sleep for the excitement of being surrounded by such an overload of strangeness, and I made up the part of the somnambulist to spook myself more deeply.

I was timid around Becky's mother, afraid of her wheelchair the way I was afraid of an iron lung. I recognized that her affliction made her unpredictable, like a baby. When she left her wheelchair, she wore a heavy leg brace and, leaning on a cane, tottered stiffly along like the Tin Man before he was oiled. She squealed whenever she was happy or annoyed or confused. She spoke only an occasional word—she could say "Becky," for instance—but in a high-pitched, cloudy, inarticulate voice, loud and verging on hysteria. I believed her hysteria sprang from her trying so desperately to communicate and failing. Nobody in the family knew how much she understood. If the stroke had impaired her intelligence, nobody could say to what degree.

She'd been an artist, strongly influenced by the Impressionists, Picasso, and Paul Klee. The walls of the old house displayed samples of her early work, painted exclusively in oils: a still life or two of geometrically radicalized fruit, lopsided sailboats floating on choppy water, a number of portraits, the subjects madcap and skewed, like harlequin costumes, only they were faces. In an eerie way, her art foretold her current predicament: her peripheral involvement with the real world, her physical self fractured and abstracted by her limitations. Unlike my own mother, who patiently copied the photographs of her children because she strove to duplicate with accuracy what she saw, Becky's mother had employed her art to bend and warp reality. Why? Because she was dissatisfied with what she beheld of reality and had the sort of confidence that made her think she could improve upon it? My own mother seemed unable to get enough of reality. She certainly never seemed to complain about it. Becky's mother's paintings roiled with complaint. I had some inkling that complaint and contrariness are what separates the artistic from the merely talented.

Despite her handicap, she still painted, although now she labored to lift a brush and glide it with any dexterity across a canvas. Her new paintings were primitive, a hodgepodge of fits and starts, dominated by sludgy crooked lines and harsh woolly-rough swabs of incongruous color. But she kept trying. Some faint echo of her former self that clearly was not damaged called out to her to try.

Becky had more independence than any girl I knew, and because of this I envied her. Her father gave her a clothing allowance of $350 a year and expected her to learn how to budget. "I have to buy everything with it," she consoled me. "Socks, underpants, hose, bedroom shoes. You'd be surprised how fast it goes. And you know something, I'd give every penny of it away if I had a mom I could go shopping with."

I was always complaining to her about my mother's limitations on how much we could spend when we went shopping. If I tried on six dresses and liked three of them, she'd let me pick one.

Becky's independence required a great deal of responsibility on her part. She made all her own doctor and dentist and orthodontist appointments and got herself where she was supposed to be, promptly, even if that meant calling a cab. The cab companies in Greensboro in the early '60s were derelict establishments. The service was unreliable, the cars shabby, and the drivers looked like escaped convicts. People who took cabs were usually recluse types who didn't drive and needed a lift to the liquor store, not privileged young ladies who lived in mansions and had clothing allowances and braces sparkling on their teeth. But Becky prevailed because she was a pragmatist and had gotten used to looking fearlessly after herself. She managed to open the door of a cab and slide across the grimy upholstery with grace and authority.

Whenever I spent the night with her, I felt wholly untethered. Her father didn't meddle in our business and her mother couldn't. We rarely associated with her three siblings. Mostly we flitted around the mansion like pixies; we slid down the banisters; we crawled up on the slate roof and straddled the attic dormers; we foraged in the larder for midnight snacks; we took bubble baths in Becky's private porcelain tub; we tried out the Mark Eden Bust Developer gadget that Becky had ordered out of a magazine, but it didn't work. Every room was big enough to cartwheel in, and so we did that. Nobody ever told us to simmer down. We got to boil over. The house was enormous and maybe just a little bit sad. And the sadness soaked up more of our glee, I suspect, than the shadowy, absorbent acres of space that seemed to exist between rooms.

Becky's father made no pretense about why he'd bought her a horse. It was to preoccupy her so that she wouldn't fritter her adolescent heart away on boys. He was a pleasant but calculating man with a soldierly demeanor. Having to look after the welfare of four children without benefit of a wife's support was his own handicap, and he struggled to offset it by implementing strict household rules and various other protective strategies. He had a peculiar sense, however, of what constituted appropriate activities for young teenage girls. One Friday night, for instance, we begged to see a gory horror movie called *Blood and Roses,* which was playing at the Carolina Theatre downtown, but he wouldn't take us. Instead he sent us to see *Splendor in the Grass,* starring the young, nubile Natalie Wood and Warren Beatty, crushing their lustful teenage bodies against one another until Natalie's mother intervened. Deprived of Warren's company, Natalie eventually goes insane. We came out of the movie wide-eyed, sobered, convinced that if a girl couldn't have sex with the boy she loved, she'd end up in an asylum.

When I compared my domestic life with Becky's, I was critical of my parents' shepherding influence, the abundant roly-poly warmth of my household, where sunlight bounced merrily from room to room abolishing all shadows and the possibilities of ghosts, where even the art my mother made lacked mystery. The eccentricities of Becky's family engaged me in the way that Barn Life did, seduced me away from the dulling satisfactions of a purely sheltered girlhood. I sometimes imagined that if I were orphaned, I'd ask Becky's father to adopt me. He managed his home like an efficient orphanage, which wasn't a bad thing in my mind at all; it was the stuff of novels.

I determined that Becky's self-reliance arose from her lack of opportunity to be ornately nurtured. Her good study habits and excellent grades, her brave rides in taxis, her punctuality, were admirable aspects of a maturity that had evolved not because her father had neglected her, but because he hadn't coddled her. I'd been coddled into a procrastinator who made Cs in arithmetic, believed every stranger— especially if he was driving a taxi—was a potential kidnapper, was habitually late and frequently whiny, all evidence that my parents had cut me too much slack.

The only place I outshone Becky was at the barn. She was not one to willfully jeopardize her own safety. Perhaps her father had admonished her that if she broke her arm, she'd have to set the bone herself or pay for the cast out of her clothing allowance. Whatever the source of her caution, it undermined her confidence as an equestrian.

I never had the impression that Barn Life offered her the same escape and solace it offered me. Taking care of a horse seemed more duty than joy to her, another load of chores. I don't think she doted on her horse the way some of us did. After all, her horse was her father's prescriptive antidote to ward off her interest in boys, but Becky always liked boys better than horses.

Her horse, Cricket, was a speckled dun mare who resembled Buttermilk, the famous Trigger's stablemate. Cricket's distinction was that Becky's father had bought her when she was pregnant and she'd soon given birth to a dusty black foal in her stall one day while all of us were at school. Becky named the colt Dr. Pepper, and for a summer he tagged after us wherever we rode. I mostly remember our annoyance with him when, on one occasion, he nosed his way into the feed room and knocked over a bucket of blackberries we'd spent hours picking. He ate them all. After Dr. Pepper was sold, Cricket turned sullen and vindictive. This is how we later explained Becky's accident, not that we'd been at fault.

On school days, we probably didn't arrive at the barn until four o'clock. After we'd groomed the horses and mucked out their stalls, there wasn't much daylight left for riding. Whereas Becky would have been content to ride in the big pasture, I always lobbied for a trail ride or a trip along the shoulder of either Friendly or Jefferson Road, riding through the suburbs, showing off my cowgirl freedoms and skills.

We could ride up to the Guilford College Texaco station any afternoon we chose, zigzagging between cars stuck in five o'clock traffic, waving to the drivers. Nobody would tell us that it was too close to supper for a candy bar. We'd dismount, sling our reins over a picket fence, then amble toward the station's vending machines like desperadoes come to town to visit the saloon. Nobody told us to wash up. We could chomp our food with our mouths open without reprimand. The horses, chewing sideways with grass-stained lips and rattling their bits, seemed a chorus of approval.

But even at the most triumphant heights of our journeys, Becky would frequently glance at her watch to check the time. It was an endearing habit only to the adults who depended on her, a gesture suggesting that she was a girl profoundly enslaved by duty and routine. Habitually checking her watch, she revealed an adultlike preoccupation from which no amount of horseplay could distract her. Time was her martinet, not her sidekick.

I'm sure we were running late that afternoon. We'd ridden to Quaker Village Shopping Center, tied our horses to a bicycle stand, and chugged milkshakes at the drugstore soda shop. I'd probably made us late on purpose, because my darker side was forever trying to tempt Becky away from her obligation to be home by six o'clock sharp. I wanted to blunt the sharpness because, spoiled myself by rules that were fuzzy, I imagined the sharpness that marshaled Becky's compliance as a kind of evil weapon held at the throat of childhood.

I'd talked her into agreeing to ride with me to the drugstore, but she'd urged us to trot most of the way so that we'd make better time.

On the return trip, she suggested that we canter. It was risky cantering along the narrow shoulder of a busy street. Heavy distracting traffic rushed past in both directions, but a horse might also shy for reasons a rider might not anticipate. My horse had shied before at the flipped up red flag on a mailbox, at somebody's lost mitten lying on the sidewalk, at a glinting piece of tinfoil in the ditch, at a man holding a garden hose. The faster you rode, of course, the less likely you would be to glimpse unfamiliar sights that might cause a horse to jump track and unseat you.

We knew very well that from the moment we led them out the paddock gate, our horses dreamed of return, of being nestled in their stalls, unsaddled, grinding supper portions of oats with their big unbridled teeth. That we pointed them in the direction of comfort and encouraged them to hurry couldn't have pleased them more.

I was in the lead that afternoon as we headed home, alert to the possibility of a runaway and tugging mercilessly on my reins. My horse was the queen of speed, a real dragster, and I rarely trusted her to behave. Cricket, on the other hand, had always been a drowsy, sluggish, matronly animal. Still fat from her pregnancy, she lacked the wiliness and vigor for long-distance running—or so we thought. That afternoon, however, Becky might just as well have been gouging her with spurs the way Cricket lit out.

It took all my strength to restrain my horse from joining the race. Within a minute, they'd created such distance between us that my horse forgot she'd been a contender and I relaxed my grip. Far ahead I watched Becky and Cricket vanish dreamily around a curve as if they were attached to a carousel. I may have been concerned but not alarmed. I thought Becky knew what she was doing. Didn't she always know, minute by crisp minute, what she was doing? I thought that she'd entrusted Cricket with expedient return, that Cricket was her ally against me and my dawdling. They were partners in punctuality is what I thought.

Becky hadn't shouted for help, not that victims of runaway horses ever did. It was an experience you endured solo, a horror that, once set in motion, wasn't over until the horse decided.

When we rounded the curve that had obscured Becky and Cricket, I saw a traffic jam in front of the Phillips 66 service station where we sometimes bought oatmeal cookies and bottles of Royal Crown. A few cars had pulled off the road, and a man was directing motorists around an obstacle in the road. From my vantage point, it looked like some dusty brown burlap feed sacks had fallen out of a truck. Then, as I was squinting to see more clearly, one of the feed sacks struggled upward and transformed itself into Cricket. By the time I arrived at the scene of the accident, a man wearing a suit, probably on his way home from the office, had led Cricket to the side of the road, and a number of people who'd stopped to help hovered over Becky, who sprawled unconscious, flecked with blood, in the middle of Friendly Road. I remember that she lay on her back, facing the sky with closed eyes, and that she had on a white shirt still sharply creased by a mangle-proficient ironing job. All I was good for was identifying her and remembering her home phone number. Beyond offering that information, I stepped tearfully aside and let the adults take over. One of them used the phone at the Phillips 66 station to call an ambulance. Another called Becky's residence and was informed that Becky's father was out of town on business. I just stood there, meek in the face of disaster, disbelieving, inept. Somebody gave me Cricket's reins to hold. My own horse had left the scene and galloped back to the barn on her own. The entire left side of Cricket's neck and withers had been skinned raw by the fall and she was bleeding. But the fact that she gazed with a dingy remorseless stupidity into the crowd who attended to her fallen mistress made me hate her. She was a beast after all—self-absorbed, a flagrant opportunist, a bungler and a clod; her ears pricked up only at the sound of her own name, not Becky's.

I overheard an eyewitness say that the pair had not been hit by a car, that the runaway horse had lost her footing as she galloped across the concrete apron of somebody's driveway. She'd fought against the fall in that scrambling cartoon shuffle of slipping on a banana peel before her legs cartwheeled out of control and she skidded on her side into the road. There were two types of concrete any child could readily identify: the coarse, porous kind that built sidewalks and roads and the slate-smooth concrete that slickly facilitated the speedy unimpeded glide of roller skates. The school slabs, where we played our ball games or hopscotched or skated, were made of this refined concrete, but it was also a popular choice for garage floors and some driveways. Cricket's horseshoe skid marks were etched in the pearly concrete like a wildly dramatic celebrity signature.

I must have handed Cricket's reins to someone else and slipped away from her. The proximity made me feel like her accomplice in this disaster. I was eager to move closer to Becky, although I was terrified of her, the paleness of her face, the blood, the moaning. "It's me, Becky. It's Mar," I said.

"Where's Cricket?"

"Cricket's okay. She's more worried about you than herself."

"What's happening?"

"They've called an ambulance."

"Where am I?"

"You fell off Cricket into Friendly Road. You've had a bad accident, but you're going to be okay. Keep still." I didn't know she would be okay (it would take more than one hundred stitches to patch her up), but I said it just as the adults in my life had said it in the midst of crisis, as much to calm themselves as the person they attended. I picked up one of her hands instinctively and held it the way my mother would have held mine.

"What time is it?" Becky asked. "I have to be home at six o'clock sharp."

About this time, the adults who encircled us parted to let someone through: a slender, blonde, tender-faced angel who smelled like L'Aire du Temps perfume, my mother's distinctive fragrance of choice.

How had she known to find us here? No one had phoned her. Some sixth sense mother's mandate had rerouted her. On her way to the barn to pick me up she'd seen an ambulance and she'd followed it. Since the day she'd become a parent, there hadn't been a moment's respite of guaranteed safety for the children she loved. She had never, even for a split atom of a second, taken our well-being for granted.

I remember that Becky's face pinkened once she recognized my mother's presence. She opened her eyes and smiled. How abandoned I felt when my mother climbed into the ambulance to ride with Becky to the hospital, but how proud of her for knowing exactly what to do, what to say, for dismantling the icy lonesomeness of fear wherever she showed up, for being a warm and abiding force in our uncertain world, for silently calling our bluff. I deserved to be left in the dust with the miscreant Cricket. I deserved to figure how I'd get home on my own.

METAPHORS AND PIES

The Heartfelt Home

BECAUSE I CONTINUE to live in the town where I grew up, I have visual access to my former childhood homes. Despite commercial encroachments, all four of them survive, updated and well maintained. At least two, by current market standards, are as pricey as castles; neither my parents nor I could afford to buy them today. The house which in the 1950s hosted our rowdy tumble, has since been owned by quiet retired couples and gives me such a cold shoulder when I drive past that I'm certain my family wore out its patience the same as its rugs. Renovations to the first house we lived in have so gussied up its original simplicity that, with its flowery wrought-iron garnishments, it looks embarrassed—like a plain woman sporting a grandiose hat.

I've returned to only one of these houses—by invitation—and felt oddly displaced. I behaved the way I act at high school reunions: gushy about change, when change rarely feels any better than compromise. I'm afraid that I sat pining for evidence of my long-scattered family in rooms that were no longer meant to accommodate our quirks.

In retrospect, the houses of our childhood seem more like guardians, living breathing relations, than forms of shelter, and returning to them, we dread witnessing their adaptability. To discover that our secret hideouts have been claimed for another's purposes makes us feel not only dispensable but betrayed. Knowing a house well and forming an attachment to its atmosphere and spirit is one of our earliest experiences with intimacy.

It's that intimacy with place—the sense that a house will share with us its secrets as well as its blessings—that we long for as adults and that we seek to recapture in the homes we eventually buy. Why are the houses of our adult lives never quite as influential as the ones that nurtured us as children? Perhaps, because we are responsible for their mortgages and upkeep, we view them more as burdens than sanctuaries. Creating a feeling of "homeiness" is a conscious task; we just don't fall into the feeling like we did as children. What *does* make a house a home? Perhaps only a child can tell us—or memory.

I've been growing up in Greensboro, North Carolina since about 1950, when my father, a native North Carolinian, returned to settle. For a while we lived on Aberdeen Terrace in a small rented two-story white frame house. The house had a grumbling coal furnace that my father patiently stoked each morning before he went to work. This was the house that had fig trees in the back yard. There was a boy in the neighborhood named Rudolph Gibbs, memorable because he had a name like the famous reindeer and a sister, Carolyn, whom my mother was always praising for her good manners. The Aberdeen Terrace house is the one in which I recuperated from red measles, my fever cooled hourly by alcohol rubdowns. My baby brother received shots of gamma globulin there—a word that still spooks me and globs in my mouth. I would have rather suffered the measles than those shots.

We owned our first TV on Aberdeen Terrace. I remember watching *I Love Lucy* while my mother vacuumed. I remember the vacuum cleaner: it resembled a bomb being towed on a sled.

That was the house where I slept with my entire record collection every night. My father recalled that when I tossed in my bed, all the records clattered out, making such a racket that he often shot up in the dark, thinking he'd heard burglars. I remember that I had a little plastic tote in the shape of a pumpkin, and that I set on one of our heat grates and the pumpkin melted. I don't remember my mother getting mad. Mostly she sang a lot and kissed my father while they did dishes.

I loved the neighborhood there. We had sidewalks and lots of trees. There was a crab apple tree and a pussy willow. There was a boy who took his pet rabbit on walks. Around the corner, Lois and Wallace Wolfe trained little dogs instead of children and taught the dogs a repertoire of tricks. The dogs had even better manners than Carolyn Gibbs. Mike Cole lived across the street: both he and his mother talked like they had head colds, or maybe adenoids. I liked the word *adenoids,* although I didn't want them. Some people had theirs taken out, like tonsils. It was a popular operation, a remedy of some sort that's rarely performed today. It seemed back then that somebody was running for president named Adenoid Stevenson.

We didn't live in the Aberdeen Terrace house for more than two or three years, but I retain a strong impression of its borrowed, dog-eared grace. I recall that the house faced east, and the front rooms were butter-colored in the morning, their windows swagged with white nylon curtains as thin as cobwebs. The hardwood floors were splintery and warm. There weren't any rugs; you could take running leaps and slide a long way in your socks—or if your pajamas had feet. A staircase ascended to a landing where I liked to sit, peeking through the knobby balustrades, and spy down at the adults.

Mother was glad to leave Aberdeen Terrace. "That house was cramped," she often said after we were gone. But I don't remember it that way. I remember it as offering me plenty of space for dashing and tumbling and whooshing down the banister. At night, in the dark, the house felt so big that to get to my parents bedroom in the wake of a nightmare required the dogged courage of a pioneer.

I loved the comfort of that house. It wasn't the sort of house any-

body acted nervous or prissy about. It catered specifically to my ram-
bunctiousness, and its familiarity, like soft flannel, provided the sort
of nurture that belies shabbiness.

Our second home, which my parents built, was in a lush new suburb
called Starmount Forest. I remember going out to the lot to tag trees
we wanted the bulldozer to spare.

The yard was spacious, like a small shady park, with room for
a swing set, a playhouse, a dog lot, a lemonade stand, kickball and
croquet games, and my mother's snapdragons. I remember the yard
almost better than the house. I was in the heyday of my tomboyhood
and the house alone could not possibly have contained my daredevilry.

I had my own bedroom in Starmount Forest. The walls were
painted salmon pink, a color I will forever associate with privacy because I discovered the joys of such, holed up in my bedroom, writing
my first stories or saturating myself with Nancy Drew and Lois
Lenski books.

In this house I feasted on Saturday television: Roy Rogers and
Hopalong Cassidy and Wild Bill Hickock and Sky King, the flying
cowboy. We watched television in a dark little den on a small black-
and-white set that was always missing its tuning knobs because some
child had wrenched them off.

The years spent in Starmount Forest were dominated by invention:
my first bowl of snow ice cream was eaten there; the best Halloween
costumes I ever wore were assembled by my mother there; there was
a picture window in the living room, and on frosty mornings we
scratched elaborate murals with our fingers on the glass; one Christmas morning we found sleigh bells that Santa had dropped in the
front yard—my father verified their authenticity; we turned the
swings of our playset into superlative horses, using bath towels for
saddles and my father's silk neckties for reins.

On moving day, I remember, I ran dramatically from room to

room, in a swoon of regret, kissing every wall goodbye. The house had always felt like a land of plenty, and we had not expected to leave it any more than my mother had expected to have another baby.

To accommodate our increase, my parents built what they referred to, after every meeting with the architect, as their Dream House. Everybody expects to live in one eventually, and my parents were no exception.

It was tremendous, crowding its small treeless yard with a cool, classic elegance we were always a little uncomfortable with. The house didn't seem to need us. Despite our noisy numbers, we couldn't seem to fill it up. The big square rooms, some of them tiled in linoleum to cut costs, seemed to echo the disappointments of dreams falling short. There was too much dependence on overhead lighting, rather than lamps, so that the house never felt cozy; it glowed with the high dry cheerless light of motel rooms.

Still, there was poshness and convenience: an intercom, an asphalt driveway as black and shiny as patent leather, a built-in charcoal grill beside the stove, acres of cantaloupe-colored Formica in the kitchen, two fireplaces, central air, a laundry chute, a spiral staircase, and walk-in closets far grander than my salmon pink bedroom in Starmount Forest.

We tried to liven the place up a bit. My brothers invented a game whereby they dressed in football helmets, strapped pillows around their chests for padding, then shot one another down the spiral staircase in cardboard boxes like makeshift bobsleds. We spooked each other with ghostly wails over the intercom late at night. For a biology project, we turned one of the walk-in closets into a lab and raised, etherized, and dissected white mice.

Still, the house shrugged us off. The cherry tree my father planted in the front yard as a memorial to his own father died. My parents kept postponing buying furniture for the living room—perhaps the earliest sign that they had built beyond their means. After we'd moved to the old genteel weathered house in Sunset Hills, I overheard my mother telling a friend that attempting to decorate the Dream House had been like trying to furnish Mammoth Cave.

I was seventeen when my parents bought the white two-story brick house on the corner of Ridgeway and Madison in Sunset Hills. The real estate agent had encouraged my parents to think of the house as "having possibilities." A bargain, it was in desperate need of renovation and repair. On moving day, my mother sat in the hallway on a pile of unpacked crates and wept.

But for all its dilapidation, from the moment I saw this house I knew I was home. How did I know this? Tall and handsome, tucked in a grove of towering oak trees, the house possessed both charm and dignity. A little ragged around the edges, sure, but it was a house that was not ashamed of its history. Its stairs were garrulous with creaks; the hinges of its doors and cupboards sang squeaky songs. There was a glass pantry and a carved mantel and frosted window panes in one bathroom. The walls were of cool, fragrant plaster. Outdoors, a flagstone path meandered through old-fashioned plantings that one's grandmother might have tended.

Something about the house, something sunny and possible, reminded me of our beginnings on Aberdeen Terrace, when my father had not complained about the necessity of shoveling coal, nor had my mother fussed over my pumpkin tote melting on the heat grate. This house in Sunset Hills, settled and worn, overgrown and outgrown by the family before us, felt patient—that's what it was. It was in no hurry to be anything other than what it had always been: a graceful shelter, a house to come heartfelt home to.

On the day we moved in, before she'd unpacked the first dish, my mother wiped away her tears and strolled around the living room, picking out the spot where the Christmas tree would stand. It was August. One normally did not think of Christmas trees then. But my mother was thinking of them. The house spoke to her, she said, and told her that thinking of Christmas trees and where to place them would cheer her up.

You always know that you are home when a house speaks to you— and they do speak, the best of them.

The house told me to take a spin down the long curving banister, and even though I was seventeen, I could not resist such a friendly invitation.

Why I Did Not Go to Syracuse

FIRST OF ALL, I never expected the Search Committee to call. Having never been tenured, having hopped from one teaching slot to another, I thought of myself as an academic migrant worker. The entire application process made me feel beggarly, rootless and peripheral. And so when Syracuse actually phoned me for an interview, I was suspicious. I felt disadvantaged by my southern drawl, which frequently triggers in northeasterners a feeling of superiority. I thought Syracuse was calling me for all the wrong reasons, that Affirmative Action had mandated a certain number of southerners for scrutiny. Southerners *are* a kind of ethnic group, you know. Perhaps I was their token cracker. I can say with some authority that many English departments are not known for their humanitarianism. (I once shared an office with a fellow migrant who was paid so poorly for his overloaded freshman composition courses that, in order to make ends meet, he sold blood to a plasma center every few weeks.)

The Search Committee had decided to fly me up to Syracuse for an extensive interview, if I were willing, the caller said, if I were still interested in the position. It was a *position*, not a job. I didn't know what to say, feeling disoriented by the thrill of being genuinely courted. I couldn't very well have said that I was shocked by the call, that, actually, it was sort of a *lark,* my applying to teach creative writing at Syracuse. I'd flipped through the AWP Job List, noting vacancies at colleges nationwide, and I'd circled only the plummiest jobs, the long shots, the jobs with excellent salaries and benefits and humane teaching loads. I didn't know one soul on the faculty at Syracuse. The reputations of certain faculty who had preceded me—Raymond Carver, to name but one—were daunting. I had no influence there, no insights into university politics. No persons there had previously identified themselves as fans or owed me any favors.

In my stammering reply, I think I all but questioned their integrity. It would have been like me to have bluntly asked, "Why me?"

"By the way, we've read your books," the committee spokesperson volunteered, "and we were impressed." So there it was: a rare instance of guileless success. I swooned, my heart aiming North. It was the purest invitation I have ever received.

A good number of scholarly women I know tend to dress up in shapeless dresses and scuffed leather shoes, run over at the heels, with Pilgrim buckles. Their slips show. They wear stockings with multiple runners. It might be more appropriate to blame their restrictive salaries, but I suspect that they simply don't think much about fashion, that it's their intellects they take pleasure in grooming. The nattiest tend to sport conservative suits in somber colors, manly tweeds. I've observed them at Modern Language Association conventions looking virile and shrewd, while I wisp joblessly past, wearing the most unpolitically correct of colors: pink.

When I asked tenured female colleagues at the college in Virginia where I was then teaching what I should wear to a serious northeastern tenure-track interview, they all insisted upon a suit, but something prim and Lois Lane-ish rather than man-handler chic with giant shoulder pads. I did not own a suit of any kind. One student, who happened to hail from upstate New York, implored me to buy a new coat as well. I did not own much of a coat either.

In preparation for my interview, I preoccupied myself not with reading up on deconstructionism, but with assembling a suitable wardrobe. I mention all this fuss about the protocol of dress because I knew from a previous interview—the time I'd truly worn a pink dress—that it was possible to sabotage oneself by merely looking wrong. This had been my interview with Emory, and I'd come away from that encounter filled with regrets of having appeared too blithe and too blonde for them.

I did want Syracuse to hire me. I wasn't fooling them or myself. True, a part of me was out to prove that I could compete, that I could land such a sought-after position at a respected university. I was seeking professional validation. But I also *needed* a job, a real job that hinted at permanency down the road via tenure track. For years while my children were little, I'd contented myself with part-time teaching jobs that spared me time for writing. But in the wake of a recent divorce, I felt logistically up for grabs. My ex-husband and I had opted for a custody arrangement that equally split our responsibility for the welfare of our sons. To supplement my writing income, teaching was no longer an agreeable option, but mandatory.

I flew up to Syracuse near the end of February. The weather in North Carolina was balmy, and I remember feeling wistful as the plane rose into a vivid, cloudless sky. No wonder that it had been years since I'd bought an overcoat. In my neck of the woods, forsythia and jonquils were always blooming by Groundhog Day. Everyone had warned me that I would probably run into snow, that the annual snowfall in Syracuse was around 180 inches.

Normally I love flying. I always request a window seat so that I can press my forehead to the glass and marvel. No telling what explanations for my travels I've narrated to strangers sitting beside me, for there is something about flight that inspires me to reinvent my life. But I was pokerfaced on the flight to Syracuse. This was a business trip, a mission, not a joyride. Throughout the cabin, soberly dressed patrons of nonstop jet service to New York figured their strategies on laptop computers or read the *Wall Street Journal.* Nobody gazed dreamily out windows, including me. I flipped open my copy of a Norton anthology of short fiction and reread a story by Tobias Wolff, one of the men scheduled to interview me.

A graduate student, thin and pale as a soda straw, hollow-cheeked like D. H. Lawrence, met my plane. Actually he was not a graduate student. He just bore a strong resemblance to the ones I have known, the kind who sell blood. He'd been entrusted with the task of transporting me to my lodgings, where I would be handed over to a bona fide Search Committee member. He possessed the cheerful and ingratiating manner of somebody low down on the departmental totem pole. Like me, he was used to teaching part-time. He filled gaps when professors went on sabbaticals, and he was often called at the eleventh hour when an overload of students required the creation of an additional class. An academic troubleshooter, that's what he was. Our ranks are legion. He had a family—he removed an infant carrier from the passenger seat. Bales of unmarked freshman composition papers thumped around in the back of the car. He drove a banged-up Japanese compact with a coat hanger jammed in the radio antenna socket. (A coat hanger provides an excellent makeshift antenna until you can afford the real thing.)

Oh my god, like every last one of us, he was writing a novel. If I'd been him I would have hated me. Here he was, a favorite son of Syracuse, his older children settled in school here, himself the recipient of an advanced degree and numerous publications in noteworthy journals, and yet he was not a contender for the job I sought? I asked him why not.

"Well, for starters," he said, "they want a woman."

"I've heard that one a few times myself," I said sympathetically, "but in my case, it's usually prefaced by *minority.*"

"Also, I'm much too available," he said.

We laughed. I knew exactly what he meant, what a liability availability often was. I'd never been hugely successful in acquiring long-term employment in my own backyard. The year before, I'd applied to teach at the university in my hometown and was later told by a friend who teaches there that my application was passed over because I wasn't deemed exotic enough. There was a relative of Calvin Trillin's on the Search Committee and his heart was set on a departmental renaissance. It was hoped that the university would be able to shed its provincial status if search committees would avoid regional hiring. I was too known a quantity, my accent too familiar, a local yokel, accessible, and in their opinions, a riskless and unimaginative choice.

Doug Unger, the person with whom I'd previously spoken on the phone, waited in the hotel lobby, smoking a cigarette. He greeted me enthusiastically, chatty and earnest in an Alfalfa kind of way. Doug clarified billing arrangements with the desk clerk, appropriated a room key, and led the way upstairs. After we'd appraised the room reserved for me, he outlined my itinerary, then advised me to rest. He would return with a colleague in a couple of hours and take me out for supper.

After he left, I rang up my best friend back in North Carolina. "What am I doing here?" I said. "This feels very strange. Is this me? I mean, they're treating me like I'm Flannery O'Connor or somebody."

"Why shouldn't they be nice to you if they want you to teach there?"

"Why do they want *me* to teach here? They could get anybody."

"Why should they settle for just anybody when they could have you?"

"They're just *too* nice. They're behaving like southerners," I lamented. "Maybe this is really a crummy place to teach and all their best people are starting to ditch so they're having to dip below the Mason-Dixon line for replacements because we wouldn't know Down There what's going on Up Here."

"Get a grip."

"You wouldn't believe the schedule they've mapped out for me. Tonight Doug and Tobias are taking me to dinner. Then I have to teach their writing workshop—right in front of them. I didn't know I was going to have to teach in front of anybody."

"You'll do fine."

"I've never taught in front of anybody before."

"Only about a trillion students."

"I mean other writing teachers. Oh, you know what I mean. God, I'm a nervous wreck. I might have to start smoking again. Doug Unger smokes."

"When do you give your reading?"

"Tomorrow. Tonight I teach the workshop, then we go out with all the students so that I can chat with them and they can report back to the committee about whether or not I'd fit in, stuff like that. I know they're all spies."

"Relax," my friend said.

"I'm costing them a fortune. What if they offer me the job and I don't take it?"

"Then you'll have to reimburse them for all their trouble."

"I will? Do people do that?"

"It was a joke. Jeez. Your sense of humor."

"I'm beginning to worry that I brought all the wrong clothes. There's not a speck of snow, but everything I brought looks so pastel and cheerful."

"Just as long as you nixed all the pink."

"Maybe my clothes look too bright because it's so cloudy here, what do you think? Everybody up here seems dressed up to go to a funeral—lots of black. Maybe the novel really *is* dead."

She laughed.

"Tomorrow night, they're having this banquet for me. The Search Committee, the writing faculty, the English department chairman— they'll be there. And get this: with the exception of one committee member—and *she* can't come—they're all men. Does that tell you anything?"

"Yes it does," she said. "It tells me that you're probably going to get this job."

After we hung up, I stared out the window of my hotel room for a long time. It wasn't as if I had a compelling vista of Syracuse and could contemplate what my life would be like should I decide to move there, buy a house, and settle in. My view was of a parking lot.

It might have been any parking lot in America. All the cars were recognizable models. Bits of trash scuttled across the pavement along with an occasional passerby. Beyond the parking lot stood a cinder-block wall, and beyond the wall, trees edged a dimming sky with the prickly lacework of bare branches. I couldn't tell what sort of trees they were, only that they reminded me of the debonair Bradford pears that grew along the fence in my own back yard. I might have been anywhere—even home.

Gazing into the parking lot as if it were a flattened crystal ball, I could convince myself that I would fit into this community just fine, that there would be no major adjustments, no homesickness, and that one situation was as good for me as any other. I could convince myself that I was able to do it: really move to Syracuse, away from my southern homeland, that I would be able to make long-lasting friends, inspire trust and respect among new colleagues, advance the education of my children in smart New England schools, learn to enjoy winter sports, learn about snowshoes and cross-country skiing, teach my heart out, write more books, create a home practically from scratch. I could convince myself that the wise and timely thing to do was to alight, finally, at an academic institution long enough to *earn* a reputation, that securing a good job was the first step in securing a good life.

A feeling of serenity and confidence overtook me as I stared into that idle parking lot. I knew that very soon Doug and Tobias would arrive to escort me to dinner. They would park their cars—sturdy, unfancy workhorse cars, similar to the car I drove—in that all-American parking lot, and they would hurry against the brisk weather into the lobby to greet me, and I would begin to think of them as friends rather than interrogators.

Doug had changed from jeans to corduroy slacks and a sports coat, and entering the hotel lobby, he blew on his fingers to warm them. The weather had changed, too. A wake of frosty air pursued him through the door. Tobias—or Toby, as his friends call him—wore a leather flight jacket with a brown fur collar and a sporty tweed cap. We shook hands. He was tall, robust, with a swashbuckling moustache that dragged the corners of his mouth downward so that even when he laughed, the laugh seemed vaguely cynical or melancholy. We walked to a nearby restaurant, three abreast, chatting amiably.

Among us there were few silences, even after our food arrived and we began to eat. We were all about the same age and had grown up in different parts of the country but mostly in small towns. Our educational backgrounds were similar. We discovered mutual acquaintances and caught each other up on their doings and whereabouts. Doug and I were both divorced after long marriages. Toby seemed the contented husband, coach of his sons' baseball teams and the father of an infant daughter.

We commiserated about the teaching burdens of writers, the depletion of one's own creative sap in the line of duty. But we were in accord with Randall Jarrell's devoted sentiment: that he would have gladly *paid* the university for the privilege of teaching.

Since his last book—a memoir—had made him famous, Toby was in the enviable position of teaching a reduced class load at full salary. Was Doug jealous? Would I be jealous, in time? I attempted to detect chinks in their armor of mutual regard but found none. There wasn't any reason for me to distrust them or their descriptions and assessments both of the department in which they taught and of my suitability.

By the time we left the restaurant for our walk uphill to campus, they were advising me as to the appropriateness of the material I'd chosen to read before an audience the next night. They were as outspoken and protective as my brothers might have been, vetoing an essay in favor of my reading fiction. They didn't want me to miscalculate my audience's expectations and louse up my chances.

Teaching classes late, after supper, when instead one ought to be winding down the day and giving in to the drowsy comforts of a full stomach and warm, lamplit rooms, feels vivifying and defiant. A sensation not unlike meddlesomeness accompanies putting one's coat back on and going out into the tired dark world to try to make sense of it—which is what we attempt to do in writing classes, day or night.

Any university generates an amazing intellectual night shift, and its bright fervor is infectious. I've never set off to teach a class after dark that I've not recalled the eagerness with which I departed the dinner table in the summers of my childhood, scampering across cool lawns stippled in a chenille of clover to fill my empty mayonnaise jar with captured lightning bugs.

The students in the Syracuse workshop class looked liked my students back home: meditative, haunted, irreverent. Their clothes were baggy; their jammed-to-bursting book satchels were slung over backs of chairs. Writing students are the sort who will go sockless even in inclement weather. The furtive scents of last cigarettes smoked seconds before class dragged after them into the room like tails.

I performed decently that night, but one never knows from class to class if one will be properly wired to bring light. Whether my confidence had been inspired by my hosts' conviviality or whether I'd simply dropped my inhibitions and played to everybody's expectations of exotica—because in Syracuse I was exotic—I don't know. I've always been inclined to feel looser among strangers, to ham up my act, to risk certain condemnations because, as a visitor, I won't have to hang around the aftermath of my mistakes for long.

After workshop, everybody moseyed over to the campus saloon, where we were joined by a few more faculty members. It was late and everybody looked as tired as the end of a parade. I knew that we were all gathered there, still smiling, still attempting jaunty conversation because we *had* to be, because we were engaged in the business of finding me out. I thought about Toby's wife, tending three little children all evening by herself, without his steadying company, and I felt guilty for delaying his return home.

Several women students sidled up to me at the bar. "Please come to Syracuse," one of them beseeched, taking me by the elbow as if to guide me there. "*Please.* You'd be perfect." The intimacy of her gesture was so exposed, her whisper so exaggerated that I knew she meant everyone to notice. They were all in cahoots.

"It's not that Toby and Doug aren't wonderful," another girl said. "They *are* wonderful. You guys are *wonderful!*" she called to them.

"But they aren't women," another girl said.

"Although it's not as if they don't *try* to be women, on occasion, for our sakes," said the woman who held my elbow. "But the verisimilitude is somehow lacking."

By this time, Doug and Toby had strolled over, smirking. "Relax," Doug said to them. "It's very possible that we are going to hire you a woman."

❧

It's a strange and probably universal phenomenon: when you have within your grasp something you've reached for your entire working life, you begin to question the magnitude of your desire for it, its true rank among your priorities.

Back at my hotel, in the privacy of my room, I thought deeply about what it would mean for me to move to Syracuse. There was no disputing the gains for my professional life. But what about the life of my heart? I knew that this was a terribly old-fashioned query. Just now, typing it, I heard somebody groan. I can anticipate a mass sigh of dismay from other women who might one day read this memoir, modern women on the go, jugglers extraordinaire, who will view my hesitant allegiance to professional advancement as weak and retrograde.

But when I talk about the life of the heart, I am not talking about romance. I am talking about one's off-duty life, the life lived at home, apart from the glories, satisfactions, and pitfalls of one's work. I mean the life of the *hearth,* the opportunity for being sheltered and tenderized at the end of a long day, for seeking comfort and refreshment when one leaves the office and heads home. Do you want to be returning to that home? Would you rather be heading home than not? Those who claim that their work is their life may as well be numbered among the homeless.

"Home" is rarely an abstraction in anybody's mind. It is mostly a specific place, even peculiar, with an unwavering atmosphere as palpable as broth. It smells and sounds and looks and feels a certain way that either accommodates or inhibits one's recovery from the world. How could I determine whether I would feel glad about returning home at the end of a teaching day at Syracuse? What sort of home could I make in Syracuse that would provide my children and me with a sense of nurture and familiarity as ample as we now enjoyed? Did I have the talent for making a home wherever I went? I had lived in North Carolina all my life. My children had been born there, they had grown up around an assortment of interested relatives. My mother—the sort of grandmother who will drop whatever she's doing to play a hand of poker with a bored grandson who's biked over for her company—lived right across the park from me.

Yet people with similar attachments moved every day, relocated families to dreamy new sites and began startling new routines to which everyone adjusted, given time. America has become a nomadic society, and the adult who continues to live and work in the town where she grew up is a vanishing species.

I sat there in my hotel room in Syracuse, staring glumly into the parking lot, which was now pitch black and mysterious and probably not very safe. What was lacking in me that I couldn't begin to feel a winner's sense of triumph over doubt? I was on the verge of winning a job for which many qualified and ambitious writers had applied. The benefits were tremendous, the students friendly and bright, the town attractive, its outskirts undulating toward pastoral vistas and lakes. For my two boys, there was even a basketball team with a national reputation to root for. The worst that anybody had said about Syracuse was that there wasn't much sunshine.

I slept fitfully. The next morning I dressed in a makeshift suit and went to lunch with the dean of Arts and Humanities in an old Tudor house referred to as the Faculty Club. There was thick fresh linen on the tables and cut flowers in vases and waitpersons dressed in white aprons and black ties. What did I think of Syracuse? The dean asked me eagerly. I had only high praise for Syracuse. I could not find a single fault with the town or the university or the people who lived there—except that Syracuse was not home and I was uncertain how to go about making it so.

By the end of my visit, the committee had unanimously agreed on my appointment. Even the chairman, a starchy deconstructionist, approved the selection and had suggested raising my proposed salary

and extending my appointment date by one semester if doing so
would make relocation and its attendant disorder more manageable. A
dream job was being offered to me, and how many dream jobs come
our way in a lifetime? I didn't have a writer friend or colleague who
would consider me sane if I turned Syracuse down, under the circumstances.

All my life I had been saying that I wanted to leave North Carolina,
that I believed it was incumbent upon the artist to leave home, if only
to understand home better. Not that home *ought* to be left, but that,
at some point, it *needs* to be left, as a test of courage, the courage that it
takes to live as an outsider for a while in a world that celebrates be-
longing. We tested such courage almost daily as children, thrillingly,
every time we ran into the woods.

All my life I had been saying I would leave North Carolina if only
opportunity would arise or some unavoidable summons would come.
Now that the chance for adventure had arrived, however, I was dig-
ging in, hanging back. It made sense to hang back, and yet it did not
make sense. It made sense because of the children, my worry about
uprooting them. It made sense because my ex-husband did not want
them to go.

It would be easy to blame my decision not to go to Syracuse on my
ex-husband, for the truth about joint custody is that there is less trajectory away from a flawed union than circumscription by it, and that
it tethers parents to within a vocational commuting range of one another. The state of North Carolina claims jurisdiction over the children of divorced couples—they are considered state's resources; no
judge would have permitted me to take my children away without
their father's consent.

Did I ask him for it? No. Ours wasn't an amicable divorce, and the
tone our infrequent conversations took was rarely one of accommo-
dation. I put off broaching the Syracuse matter altogether due to my
own creeping reservations. Would such a move be beneficial for my
children? If I asked him to relinquish primary custody to me, I was

committing myself to passionate argument, perhaps a legal battle. Something had checked my passion. Some hesitancy that dulled my do-or-die urgency, blunted my certainty about why I'd applied to Syracuse in the first place. Had it been some sort of self-dare, a self-administered test to determine how ruthlessly I could pursue a goal without taking other loyalties into full account? Syracuse's flattering selection had so entranced me that, for a little while, I believed my life had been miraculously streamlined, that I could travel light (and light-hearted), that there was no serious baggage I'd be hauling north.

But what if the custody obstacle hadn't existed? What if permission to travel had been granted and the children had seemed eager, excited by the prospect of 180 inches of snow annually, winter sports, proximity to the enthrallment of big cities, new friendships with Yankee children who seemed as remote as Eskimos? What if I had been granted the uncomplicated choice of going where I was most professionally cherished, of leaving the place I'd called home for most of my life and advancing my fortunes elsewhere? Would I have said yes? Wouldn't there have been tremendous shame in saying no? Would saying no have meant that I lacked courage? Even if I had discovered that I was as rootbound as a plant going nowhere but its pot, should I have felt apologetic for choosing staying over leaving?

When at last I did say no to Syracuse, I grieved for my inability to lead two lives. I said No, of course, because to leave without my children would have been unthinkable, as unnatural as a tortoise casting off its shell. There would have been no way for me to make a home in Syracuse without them.

I stayed in North Carolina, teaching as a migrant, living frugally, finishing two books, hoping to turn a corner any day and find opportunity knocking closer to home. I might have gone to Syracuse had I been a tougher, more pragmatic woman, or perhaps the sort of woman who is still toiling zestfully at work when her dependable, self-reliant children arrive home from school and let themselves in. But now and again, because of their particular frailties, my two boys seemed unhappy when the school bus let them off, and I preferred to be there, opening my arms to them.

Things changed in Syracuse, I heard. The chairmanship of the

English department passed to someone I never met. Money dried up. Doug Unger took a glamorous post at the University of Nevada at Las Vegas. The weather got worse. Recently at a party, I met a woman who teaches at Syracuse and she told me the wild tale of a faculty member throwing his cocktail in some poor student's face. "It must be somebody new they hired," I remarked, somewhat defensively. "Everybody I met was a gentleman."

Should I have told Syracuse yes? I'll never know the answer with conviction. Which, for a writer, is more fruitful: dreaming dreams or attempting to live them? I never know from day to day, as devoted to the intricate contentments of the hearth as I am transfixed by the dilemmas of my art, which I am best suited for, in temperament and spirit, which clearly gives me the most pleasure. Which finally matters most, not just to the people I love, but to the world: the making of a pie or a metaphor?

How could I have guessed that in a few years the university down the road would offer me the job of directing their creative writing program? Irony rules. We are all lightning rods awaiting impact. Number me, temporarily, among the more contented survivors, for it now appears that the storm has passed over and did not blow those pies I was cooling off the windowsills. If anything they've been transformed into just desserts.

Life is long and tricky, as silly as it is serious. Long-range intuition does not exist or I would have never written this memoir. It might now be said that I made the right choice, not going to Syracuse. It might just as easily be said that I lucked out. I might also be admonished not to feel too comfortable with my glossy new appointment, always to keep the address of the nearest plasma center in my pocket.

At Home in Snow

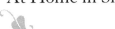

A FEW YEARS ago, I bought an old house, built during World War I: a fixer-upper with heart pine floors, glass-fronted cabinets, windows mullioned in a hopscotch pattern, a claw-footed tub, and a wrap-around front porch shaded by a monstrous oak. With its scaling paint, tilting kitchen floor, bathrooms resembling the ugly dripping disrepair of bus station lavatories, the house is still very much a work in progress. So basic my efforts at renovation, so simple the amenities, Thoreau could live in this house today and not feel like a sell-out.

The kitchen, for example, is profoundly challenged in the modern-conveniences department. I bought a secondhand GE Americana stove, electric with double-decker ovens. My used fridge came from a country salvage shop where all repaired appliances were plugged into extension cords and displayed in a pasture. Remember the old-fashioned ice cubes you froze yourself in trays? I've got them in abundance, plus one of those 1950s-style ice crushers, a little turquoise bomb-shaped gizmo, mounted on the wall. We open all cans with one of those hand-held leverish contraptions. We open our bottles on a vintage Coca-Cola opener that came with the house, attached to the doorframe of the pantry. I have no food processor. Unless you count me. For whipping up meringues and mashed potatoes I employ a Mixmaster from the 1940s. It will not be rushed, puttering at its chores with the steady, methodical determination of an antique tractor.

We have no dishwasher: instead, a metal, enamel-glazed twin sink unit flanked on either side by molded dish drains. Emblazoned like a hood ornament on the face of the unit is a red metallic sculpture of Diana, goddess of the hunt, her bow strung tightly with an arrow. Perhaps Diana dispensed with doing the dishes by shooting them to smithereens. But quite honestly, the sink—equipped with stainless steel trimmings—seems as elegant as a roadster, inspires you to get behind a pile of dishes and *drive!*

Excuse me, did I mention that we have no dishwasher? Actually there are three of them in residence much of the time: myself and two sons who are only a little less poky than my faithful Mixmaster.

This funky little kitchen is the setting of a story I want to tell about my youngest son, Sam, and how the teensiest brainstorms in life are frequently the most resonant. Eventually this story will star my Granny Cannon's meat grinder, which would probably be R.I.P. in a cardboard box in my attic if I owned a glitzy modernized Indianapolis 500 kitchen roaring out precision, technologically loaded, nonfat high-fiber vitamin-drenched food at the speed of light. Of all my clunky kitchen contraptions, my favorite is the meat grinder, clamped in dogged low-tech splendor to the end of one counter as if by true grit.

It's the first winter in our new old house. My oldest son, Rod, is away in New Jersey at choir school. The cat, Edward John Dan Henry Francis, has rooted out a nesting place in his favorite armchair, satisfied that he belongs here. (He's been running back to our old house at least once a week for months. Our former residence is located a few blocks away, beside Temple Emanuel, the synagogue; since Ed usually disappears on Friday nights, we suspect he's merely exercising the faith of his choice—but we worry.)

Tonight cold rain has spangled suddenly into snow—big, disheveled, cornflake-size bits—and Sam, my youngest son, shouts jubilantly from his bedroom to inform me. How lucky that the snow's materialized on Thursday night, one of the nights that Sam's always with me, according to the custody schedule. The fact that he's visiting on what is possibly the only snowy evening this particular year in Greensboro seems ordained by some Chief Justice in the sky. Both my boys tell me that I'm a Saturday person; their father, a Sunday sort. A Saturday grown-up will dash to the window every twenty seconds to see how much snow has fallen and will scrounge up a fire and heat up a pot of hot chocolate with marshmallows to get folks in the mood for love—love of this cantankerous, cynical, befuddling world suddenly frocked in the poetic finery of snow.

When it begins to snow in our part of the South, the television Weather Team starts filming the trajectories of individual snowflakes. They speculate rather than report. "IF the temperature continues to drop, IF bridges ice, IF school is canceled, such-and-such MIGHT happen." The Weather Team, standing alongside the bridge that's icing over even as they speak, reminds viewers to act mature about the snow, reminds us of snow's hazards. None of them have southern accents, so no wonder they think the snow's no fun. They have hairdos that, in spite of blizzard conditions, hold their shapes like igloos.

With the first televised flake, everybody rushes to the grocery store. The novel possibility of being housebound without food in the pantry is cause for gleeful panic. If it's a substantial snowfall, followed by frigid temperatures, side streets may go unscraped for days.

At the grocery stores, cashiers can hardly ring up your milk and cocoa for gazing out the windows themselves and dreaming of early dismissal. If roads begin to freeze after dark, even grocery stores will close early and send employees home. The possibility of release makes the cashiers giddy. They ring up oranges as tangerines, muffins as doughnuts, coffee as tea—and who the heck cares?

The bread runs out in an hour, along with milk and frozen pizza and popcorn. Pancake supplies dwindle. Pancakes are usually the choice celebration supper of the first snowfall at my house. Easy to make (like playing in puddles), they give Saturday people more chances to run to the window to check the pulse of the storm. Run to the window, watch while a branch loads up with flakes and a cardinal darts blood-red against the opalescence of twilit snow, race back to the skillet, flip.

I had a girlfriend when I was growing up who called her father Mr. deVile—code talk for Mr. Devil. He had a ruthless temper (and he didn't mind who knew it), was insulting to every member of his family, pushed his wife around, disowned his oldest daughter when she got pregnant in college, loathed blacks, hated Catholics and the pope, newspaper editors, Democrats, Jews—especially the owners of local textile mills, who he said swaggered around with diamond pinky rings. He thought women were a lower life form than mold; he considered the assassinations of the Kennedy brothers and Martin Luther King Jr. timely and meritorious deeds. Mr. deVile was a college-educated man and successful in business. He wasn't an alcoholic. His temper wasn't chemically induced; it was a bred-in-the-bones flaw, his heart a rumbling Vesuvius always threatening bilious spew.

But on the morning after the first snow of any given winter, Mr. deVile arose before any member of his slavish, coal-shoveling family, and he opened his door to the snow elves. The snow elves were his invention; they were minions of Jack Frost, yet more revered, more secretive, more generous, leading the march of the snowflakes. They liked to run down the chimney and warm themselves and dance around with excitement—-and who could blame them? If snow was predicted, Mr. deVile always put out a plate of food for them the night before he went to bed, and he encouraged his three children to do the same.

In the morning, if the elves had led a successful march and had found favor with their accommodations, you discovered thrilling evidence. Throughout the house in a jaunty stencil of washable white tempera (Mr. deVile said the paint was a form of meltless magical snow) ran chalky boot prints shaped like tiny spades. Up and down the walls, across the kitchen countertops, the linoleum floor, the windowpanes, tramped the mischievous stitchery of bootprints, undeniable proof of visitation.

The elves, unlike Santa or the Tooth Fairy, left no gifts, just snow, and everybody felt satisfied, even beholden. We speculated that the elves had to be real, that Mr. deVile wasn't the sort of lighthearted man who enjoyed silliness or mess. He complained about the bootprints later and made his children sponge them away. My friend waking up, her brother and sister, all three marveled at the dizzy runaround of bootprints, marveled even more at the calmness of their father slouched in his chair, drinking coffee, reading the newspaper, telling them to pipe down, to curb their excitement because it was giving him a headache, denying every time they asked that he had anything whatsoever to do with the elves, didn't believe in such nonsense, thought the whole business was pure malarkey, and which one of his young rascals would own to having made such a mess? He seemed to know what children were suckers for and how easily they forgave a parent's sins for a warm idle moment of playfulness.

Of course none of them could admit to having conjured the elves. They were baffled. It was the only time all year that they would cling rapturously on the arms of their father's broody chair. It was as if the snow elves had delivered a new father to them as well as snowfall, and they were beguiled. Outside the sharp protuberances of the landscape had grown soft and round, the pickets of all fences, blunted. Where the snow had fallen, all lay meek and lovely, ugliness blurred or entirely revised, doubt dispatched by the holy snowy light. The world, in spite of all they knew to the contrary, was wholly beautiful.

My own father reverted to boyhood whenever he got the chance, and snow provided one of those chances. He enjoyed sledding with my brothers and me, hogging the sled sometimes, treating himself to dangerous rides down swooping hills he claimed were too steep for us.

He hollered with the thrill of speed. He slicked the sled runners with a bar of Ivory soap.

Children love adults who aren't afraid of making fools of themselves, and my father was completely fearless. He participated in friendly snowball fights until, inevitably, some rowdy would cross the boundary of good sense and aim for somebody's eye. Then my father grew stern and pouty, disappointed in our recklessness. Unhappily, he realized his authority, became instantly cautionary, peeled away from the snow as if from a disguise, and was suddenly too tall for play.

He liked mobilizing early on a snowy morning, sliding his hands into a pair of gloves lined with rabbit fur. He rarely wore a hat. Although he complained about the challenge of swaddling the rear tires of his Chevrolet with snow chains, as soon as the task was completed he gloried in accomplishment. He refused to be snowbound. After all, he was a doctor in the days when doctors still made house calls. He relished being the first resident to plow exploratory tracks down our snow-erased street. We children stood at a window, waving him off. He waved back like Peary on his way to plant a flag at the North Pole. He grinned upward at the dizzying twirl of flakes; he held out his arms to the storm as if it were our mother all dressed up in lace and he was begging her to dance. We knew he'd close his office early and return home by afternoon, that most of his patients didn't have the will or stamina for cleating their tires with snow chains and venturing into treacherous weather. They would cancel their appointments. And to my father, it would seem as if the snow had the power to postpone illness for a while.

When I was in college, I attended a friend's birthday party and toward the end of the evening, when an extravagant cake ablaze with candles was toted into the room, we guests began to sing. The words of the song were familiar—I'd been singing them since childhood: "For he's a jolly good fellow, for he's a jolly good fellow, for he's a jolly good fellow, with snowberry candlelight." As I sung the final phrase, I was aware for the first time in my life that I was proclaiming a different sentiment from other well-wishers. "What did you just sing?" somebody asked.

Of course, what I should have sung was "which nobody can deny." What on earth *was* "snowberry candlelight"? my friend inquired. I'd never questioned what it was. I'd always heard—or misheard—the lyrics that way and had sung them throughout my life. The phrase hadn't seemed peculiar in the least to me. I'd associated the words with some beneficent loveliness, the sprinklings of a crown chiseled from a snowdrift. I'd imagined snowberry candlelight as some sort of tangible blessing wafting down the sky, sparkling weather falling from lucky stars, anointing the head of a jolly good fellow with ethereal frosting: the perfect miracle of warm snow.

As a kid, I did not own any serious gloves or mittens—except for my going-to-church cotton ones, prim and white as steeples. My brothers and I were domestically haphazard; garments used infrequently got mislaid. My brother Knothead was capable of losing garments as significant as coats. They frequently disappeared right off his body on his way home from school. His glasses disappeared just as often or got mangled. And so on any given snowy morning we might be able to ferret out two or three outgrown gloves, all left-handed and motheaten. While Mother scrambled our eggs and the coffee chugged away in its percolator with the glass-bubble top and Daddy hummed "The Yellow Rose of Texas" off-key while he shaved, we children began to rummage for the makeshift gear that would protect us from dreaded frostbite.

I owned a pair of thin red rubber boots. They were hand-me-downs from a cousin in Colorado. Once they'd been lipstick red, but they had faded to the exact color of Dentyne chewing gum. I insulated the boots with three or four pairs of my father's socks: hard, thin, ribbed nylon socks the drab colors of dogs, black and brown and gray. Some of them had holes in the toes. You could pull them past your

knees they were so stretchy. We used them for mittens, too. We wore
flannel pajamas under our jeans and sweaters and snow-absorbent
wool coats. Sometimes, if we couldn't find proper hats, Mother tied
our heads up in babushkas fashioned from her dressy silk scarves. My
brothers ripped the babushkas off as soon as they left the house, pre-
ferring the clang of frostbitten ears to the embarrassment of dressing
like girls.

It was knowing that we could come in from the cold at any time
we chose that made playing outside until we were nearly frozen so
glorious. We staved off shelter as long as we could; the longer we did,
the more beckoning and homespun the glow of lamps in the window.
Our mother stayed inside, patient handmaiden to our exploits, helping
us peel out of soggy clothes, drying them in the clothes dryer, helping
us button and zip back into carcoats. She heated cocoa in an aluminum
pot, sprinkled it with marshmallows, stirred up homemade vegetable
soup and stovetop fudge impaled with a candy thermometer that
looked as imposing as a syringe. Sometimes she'd make Eggs a la
Goldenrod: creamed hard-boiled egg whites sauced over toast and
sprinkled with the pollen of hard-boiled egg yolks mashed through a
strainer. Normally we ate Eggs a la Goldenrod when she and Daddy
went out for the evening—the dish was the equivalent in its day of
fast food. But on a snowy afternoon, Eggs a la Goldenrod was festive,
happy-occasion food, and she ate it right alongside us. She lay on her
stomach on the Wunda-Weave rug in the living room and drew pictures with me or played cards after I'd worn myself out with frostbite
and snow blindness and the melancholia over melting snowmen.
She'd take her biggest stew pot, fill it with tepid water and help us
unbind our feet, once and for all, from the mummification of frozen
wet socks, our feet so dead asleep we couldn't feel her touch, only observe that our skin looked as glassy as quartz and stung when we first
slid them into the water. We'd soak, stupefied by comfort, sitting in
front of a heat grate, shivering, feeling dramatically salvaged from the
cold, imagining that the lethal chill of a narrow escape was thawing
out of our bones. A minute longer outside and we might have been
victimized by gangrene. We loved to threaten and terrify ourselves,

imagining close calls with gangrene. *Gang green, gang green, with its rotting oozing sheen; you won't live to be a teen if you catch that old gang green.*

❧

After a plentiful snow, tons of the stuff, shoveled into sloppy pyramids in shopping center parking lots, would ebb for sorrowful days, sometimes weeks. Nothing was more disappointing than to watch the snow which had been so lavish in its gorgeous bluster—celebrity of all weather systems—weaken and dissolve into little gray has-been patches. What if, as a child, you awoke one morning and your strong, handsome father had turned feeble and bald and broken-down overnight? The snow that lingered on the ground was a similar phenomenon of decrepitude. It looked like the paper trash thrown out car windows, an eyesore. It bore no resemblance to the storm's quick-change artistry and dominion over all the land, its elaborate ornamentation, its natural ordinance of calm.

Now the melting leftover bits seemed as unfriendly as they were ugly. "Watch your step, you might slip," our father cautioned as we hurried out the door for school. Smirks of ice, nearly invisible, undetectably mean, caused us to walk hunched over, gingerly positioning our feet one at a time, plodding our course as if we children had ourselves turned elderly overnight.

"You know what farmers say about snow that hangs around?" our father said. "That it's waiting for more snow to join it." And we would feel cheered, searching the sky for fresh evidence of a snow cloud brewing. We thought ourselves expert at detecting imminent snowfall. The tinny smell of coldness unloosened from a milky span of sky that looked curdled, not smooth, and the faraway calls of friends seemed heaved upon dense absorbent silence. The bare limbs of trees gestured like bony hands scavenging the air for gloves. The earth was so hard that when you jumped from a swing and landed, your bones clanged: there was vibration in your skin, clamorous resistance, no suppleness, and your feet felt broken. The sky was so swollen with white that you feared the sun might break through any moment and ruin everything.

Decades later, I imagine that I can still smell snow. I can predict its arrival by the posture of trees, a winter-ragged, blank, beseeching lawn. It's something like detecting the world's craving for garnishment and surprise. I monitor the snow as it drifts down, am disappointed if the flakes dissipate into a more shredded-looking mix of rain and sleet. I turn off the loudmouth television forecasters. *Hurry, snow!* I think. *Prove a depth unpredictable. Become the quintessential snow of the South's long, garrulous memory.* I am rooting for the snow as if it has ambition, as if it is the surplus of Heaven's kindness, an angel of mercy falling to earth feather by feather, making a miracle every place it lands.

"What's for supper?" Sam asks as we camp in front of the living room windows, watching the downward spiral of each downy pearl. Already the grass is covered, the bushes swagged in dusty shawls of the stuff. "Can we make Castleburgers?"

He always asks for them, his favorite meal, a recipe based on burgers I ate as a teenager at the Boar and Castle Drive-in, which no longer exists. The owners sold the property to an insurance company and abandoned hordes of fans pining for the distinctive flavors of Castleburgers, buttery fried panbread, jelly rolls, and uniquely tart limeades called green drinks—none of which have been commercially replicated by newer establishments. Boar and Castle steak sauce is still manufactured, available in pricey little bottles at grocery stores throughout the state, and is the necessary ingredient of the burger I have reinvented and addicted my sons to.

Castleburgers (about 6)
    1 lb. lean ground beef
    1 med. onion, chopped and mixed with beef
    1/2 cup Boar and Castle steak sauce, mixed with beef and onion
    A shake or two of salt and a dash of pepper

Form hamburger patties (thin) and fry in buttered skillet until medium-well done. Meanwhile, warm any inexpensive hamburger bun (the flatter and plainer the better—and more reminiscent of the originals). Swab the interior of the buns *unstintingly* in real butter (there is NO substitute). Pour generous pools of Castle sauce on the buns and warm slightly. Add patties and eat with gusto. Expect the sauce to leak all over your fingers, but that's part of the fun. My children like cheeseburger variations of Castleburgers, but this is a corruption of the form.

And why not treat ourselves to Castleburgers on a snowy night? For starters, we're out of hamburger meat. We have bottles of sauce and plenty of frozen buns, even the necessary onion—but no meat.

"Let's go to the grocery store," Sam suggests. "It'll be neat driving in the snow."

Oh God, the grocery store!

"Let's have pancakes instead," I say, but we're out of eggs and pancake syrup, so off we set, journeying into the bedlam of snowstorm shopping.

"This is fun!" Sam says, although the boulevard we travel is merely wet, the snow vanquished by the heavy swoosh of workday traffic. But our delight is in driving into the snow's frantic swarm, the darkening sky scudding over us like a dropped hive. "Think we'll have school tomorrow?"

"Oh, I'd do my homework just in case."

In the beam of our headlights, the whizzing snow polka-dots the air.

"How much do you think it will snow, Mom?" He cracks his window a little bit and takes a gulp of air. "I smell deep," he says, sniffing.

"Me, too," I say. "It's probably going to snow about a foot tonight, the biggest snow in piedmont North Carolina since all those big snows we had three Wednesdays in a row during March one year when I was in junior high school. It snowed so much that year that the snow stayed on the ground until Easter."

"Do you wish it would snow that much again?"

"Absolutely."

"What if it never stopped snowing?"

"Suits me."

"Me, too."

"During the winter that it snowed three Wednesdays in a row," I tell him, "it got so cold that the water in Little Lake Euphemia froze over. It was a pond in our neighborhood at the edge of the woods, and all us kids went ice-skating."

It occurs to me, as I relate the story, that the most astonishing detail is that we southern kids owned ice skates. Why did we own them? What was the chance of our ever putting them to good use? We'd all seen the Ice Capades and had developed a certain admiration for figure-skating, but those of us who asked for ice skates for Christmas, and received them, tended to keep the skates boxed, like buried treasure. On occasion we'd go skating at the Coliseum, which maintained an ice rink, open to the public, during the winter ice-hockey season. Generally the company was thuggish there, and our mothers complained about the inconvenience of the drive. We were terrible skaters, clumsy and panicky about falling. We'd thought of ice skates as a means of transportation to another dimension; I think we actually thought that wearing skates would make us graceful and serene. The professional skaters we'd observed on television twirled as lithely as ribbons. Their skates bore them like pedestals. Silky little skirts no bigger than scarves fluttered and lapped at their thighs. Handsome men danced them over the ice and lifted them like batons.

When word got out that Little Lake Euphemia had frozen over, we were no less amazed that we'd had the foresight to own skates, that we were prepared to enjoy this miracle to the fullest. We congratulated ourselves. It was as if, all along, we'd been on some secret wavelength with Nature.

I remember that some older kids built a fire on the bank of the pond and that only we girls had ice skates. The boys clomped and skidded in their boots and tried to kick holes in the ice. I don't recall any of our parents venturing down to the pond to test the solidity of

the ice. Adults rarely lorded over us outdoors; they occupied foggy—
if any—presence on the peripheries of such idylls.

Inside the grocery store, we discover that not only has the store run
out of pancake mix, syrup, eggs, and orange juice, it's run out of hamburger meat as well. "Never mind," I say, selecting a large package of
beef chunks for stewing. "I just had a brainstorm."

It takes a good half hour to wait our turn in line to pay for the beef.
By the time we arrive home, snow swings from the sky steadily, like
swishing curtains of glitter. The front lawn glows white. The house
looks tucked in.

In the kitchen, I unfasten the parts of my grandmother's vintage
meat grinder, wash and reassemble it. Beneath the little steel trumpet
from which the ground meat will tumble, I spread a sheet of waxed
paper. "Now watch," I tell Sam. In short order we've ground the
chunks into scribbles of pink meat from which we sculpt a half dozen
hamburger patties.

"Cool," Sam says. Above his head hangs the cross-stitch sampler
my mother made for me years ago: MAKE IT DO, WEAR IT OUT, USE IT
UP, DO WITHOUT, it reads, cheering us on to the victories of innovation.
Both my mother and my grandmother would understand this moment, the pleasure Sam and I take in our resourcefulness. Both could
walk into my bare-bones kitchen and feel immediately at home, inspired to make a twelve-egg angel food cake here, nothing wasted,
nothing lost. My son observes how simple hand-me-down devices can
save the day. The handle on the meat grinder is long with a wooden
bead for a grip, patchily lacquered in black paint. It feels to me that
we are scrolling back the years with each rotation.

After supper, after the dishes are put away and the world is thor-
oughly dark, we bundle up to take a walk. Sam scampers ahead, but I
lag, lifting my chin to the sky, feeling cold little sparklers of snow
against my skin. I walk backward, against the wind, observing our
house in its bonnet of snow, its windows leaking light so warm I feel

the urge to run back into the yard and stand in a patch of lamplit snow, of snowberry candlelight.

"What are you looking at?" Sam calls.

"I'm watching for signs of life."

"Inside our house? But we're here."

"We're here *and* we're there," I say. "I'm looking for the life that continues even with us gone. The life of old meat grinders." I laugh because it does sound silly.

"You talk like one of the Elements," he says. The Elements are what he calls the elementary-aged children at his school, now that he's advanced to sixth grade.

"Wonder what that old meat grinder does when we're not around. Wonder who it talks to."

"You're crazy, Mom!" he shouts, plopping down to make a snow angel.

This is the first time I've seen our house in snow, and all I can think of is how much we would be missing if we didn't live there. Like a bright planet the snowstorm bore to earth, the house has a new gravitational pull on me. I forgive its drippings and crookedness, its warped window casements and crazed plaster ceiling. To stand outside it in the cold whirring darkness, to imagine the warm life that awaits me back inside, I feel more spy than inhabiter, a visitor to a place where someone, perhaps a grandmother, is indoors stirring soup. It's as if what's valuable has to be sneaked up on, relished at a distance, withheld, imagined from the point of view of an outsider, to be fully appreciated. I would like very much to live in that house, I think; but, of course, I already do.

"Mom!" Sam calls to me across the distances of snow and memory and uplifting evening air. "Come on! Hurry up!"

Medium Cool

IT'S NEARLY SUPPERTIME. Miraculously I'm not out in traffic, driving somebody to a guitar or piano lesson. I'm not helping anybody jar insects for a biology project or dashing over to Office Depot to buy Wite-Out for all the mistakes we've typed into a procrastinated research paper. I've found an idle millisecond and have plopped on the living room sofa to enjoy it with a book in my hand. Actually I've got four books at the ready, fanned out like playing cards. I've a tendency to binge when I've got the leisure.

Such self-indulgence is a milestone in my evolution. I've been a Mom-pod for so long, a virtual volvox of child-linked chores and obligations (and, yes, the occasional pleasure), that I honestly don't expect to read more than a sentence or two without interruption. My young teenagers seem to need me in higher maintenance dosages than they ever did as babies. Mostly my job is to soothe or refresh. I'm the human equivalent of Tic-Tacs or Aspergum, the token, if uncool, legal substance in their lives. They consider most of the advice I have to offer pure placebo.

One of the books I'm clutching is *Crime and Punishment*. I noticed it listed on my older son's summer reading list, and I've decided that we should read it together. As sons grow up, there seem fewer activities that they can share with their moms. Mostly moms serve as cooks, chauffeurs, and human memos. So I'm thinking that reading *Crime and Punishment* with Rod will provide a little intellectual bonding, some conversation that doesn't revolve around his strategies for skateboarding or attending a distant 311 concert.

Anyway, I'm leafing leisurely through the book, *daydreaming* about reading it, relishing the quiet, enjoying the way the late afternoon sunlight slants through colored glass bottles I've arranged on a window sill. I haven't lost my flair for absorbing brief but intense encounters with a richly sensory moment. How lovely to meditate on the moth-like flutterance of light on the living room floor, to bask in a windfall of calm.

Meanwhile, my fifteen-year-old, Rod, is cruising the neighborhood with his cronies. He's earned some free time. He spent the last several days involved with a massive biology project: the capturing and classifying of forty common insects. It was a gruesome sideshow of a project. I wished he'd picked the leaf assortment project, but Rod had thought that the insect collection would be easier—and more fun. Maybe because he got to torture living creatures smaller than himself with impunity? One of the most memorable insects was a handsome black stallion of a beetle, brandishing a rack of elegant antlers and conveying an indisputably suave and privileged demeanor. Trapped, he appeared as outraged as some innocent potentate accused of a crime. The way he tossed and dipped his thorny head and stamped the bottom of the jar with his forelegs made us feel as challenged as matadors.

I've reached the end of the opening sentence in *Crime and Punishment* when Rod bangs in from outside, three kids trailing him. He's the oldest among them, a ninth grader, though small for his age with a choirboy face that he may never outgrow, handsome in a preoccupied, fragile way. Trooping after him are Dallas, the high-strung sixth-grader who lives across the street, and Boom, Dallas's tall, laconic sidekick. I don't know where Boom comes from, but I'm hoping it's not from those apartments across from Latham Park Quik Mart that have boss motorcycles parked in the front yards and dead trees painted with swastikas and Dixie flags pinned over imploded screen doors to keep flies out. Behind Boom saunters a young creamy girl with bushy, fox-colored hair and blue eyes as round and velvety as pansies.

"Hey, Mom," Rod says in that slack-jawed, melancholic hipster manner that performers on MTV have elevated to the status of artsy facial protocol. His voice is changing and it slides in pitch as glibly as a harmonica. This time it's dropped two octaves toward cooldom be-cause he's got an audience. "Hey, can they come in?"

They. It sounds like a rock group or a bacterium.

"Of course," I say pleasantly. "Hello, They," I say, but nobody an-swers. "Dallas, new haircut?" I observe, and Dallas grins and nods. He's a good-looking wiry young man with a freshly shaved head, am-bitiously aping Michael Jordan, sporting a braggy pair of athletic shoes he recently bought for $80 at Crunchy Music Stuff, the hippest alter-native store in town.

I've never officially met Boom, just seen him oozing around the neighborhood. I've never been introduced to the girl, Jinx, although her reputation has preceded her because last winter, for about seven hours, my younger son, Sam, and Jinx were a couple. That means that they talked on the phone about forty times between afternoon and midnight. Then Jinx realized that it was Max, Sam's skater pal, age twelve, who lives up the street, she thought she was talking with and she promptly ditched Sam. Max was intrigued until Jinx undulated up to his house wearing a pair of tight cutoffs, twirling a lit cigarette. She was way too much woman for Max.

My mother, who raised three sons and a daughter during the late sixties, tells me woefully that, with the teenage years, I'm into the awful thick of things.

As if I haven't noticed the awfully thick metallic raging of the CDs Rod listens to. To my elderly ear it sounds like lunatics trying to gnaw and beat their way out of sealed trash dumpsters. Most of the music my sons listen to has the tympani of a major landslide. My house thumps with Rod's electric guitar plugged into a Peavey amp turned bush-hog, mowing down civilization. But even when the music's off, is there any more grating and wrecking ball of sound than adolescent male voices in competition for top howl?

Then there's the added cacophony of my nagging: "Do your home-work, turn off the Nintendo, turn down the radio, help me unload the groceries, no you can't go skateboarding until you've finished your math. Because I say so. Well, I'm not like other people's mothers, so live with it. And tell your friends to call you before eleven at night or you won't be able to accept the call. Because I say so. Because some of us may not want to answer the phone if we're trying to sleep. Toss down anything you want washed. Now. Yes, you may watch *Jeopardy,* but I wish you'd read a good book now and then. This summer you're going to be reading Dostoevsky's *Crime and Punishment.* Because the high school reading list says so. No, I don't think you're a juvenile delinquent, that's not the reason you're going to read it. I'm going to read it with you so that we can discuss it together. Won't that be cool?"

When my son brings three strangers into the house, he enters ten-tatively. That's a clue, I think, that he's not altogether comfortable among them either, that he's wooing their friendship and is, himself, on trial. He is counting on me to be on my best behavior, too. He would not object to my disappearance altogether.

They revolve into the room as distinct as weather systems. From my logistical and intellectual perspectives, this crowd looms large, storm fronts to be reckoned with. The girl, Jinx, wears bright lipstick, eye shadow, *half* a tank top. I've been told she's only eleven years old. She churns languidly around the room, the queen among three drones. Her face is absolutely passive; she pays me no more heed than if I were a stick of furniture, and I feel my hospitality warping as if this girl were hard rain through an open window.

None of these kids looks me in the eye when I greet them. I'm an obstacle they're pretending to see through: ghost mom. It's important for them to believe that were it not for parents, life would run more smoothly. Our living room fills with their urgent boredom, their cool despair—all the oxymorons of dude life. Stony gazes, attitudinal slouchings: these kids are pouty prototypes, mockups of the deeper, older trouble that they are dead-eye aiming for. They have nothing to say, even to each other, and so they agitate, bump into one another, as if to rub off the contagion of restlessness, the bummer oppression of feeling inconsequential yet thinking up nothing better to feel.

It's already 6:30. Isn't anybody thinking about supper?
They clunk up the stairs in a line dance of sullenness, following
Rod to his room. He plays electric guitar for them. It's the Rod show,
but they're not the most impressed audience he's ever played for. You
might call them ingrates. I hear somebody stumble into the acoustic
guitar he keeps propped against his bookcase. I hear somebody say,
"Shut up." "No. *You* shut up," warns somebody else. They're un-
apologetic, unanimous in their forgiveness of loutishness, at an age
when nobody is hugely nice to their friends. Nice categorizes you as a
groveler, a suck-up, a sniveling underdog. You gotta be hard, steel-
hearted, impenetrable, like the songs all say.

I need, like some retro mantra, concrete recollections of what I was
up to when I was their age. Were the times simply more innocent?
Was I really some butterfly princess never making a date with a torch?
It seems essential for me to recall every crime that I ever committed in
the name of youthful verve and stupidity, that to remember the specific crimes—not their punishments or the floundering (if measur-
able) wisdom gained from those crimes—will help me to salvage and
protect my waning tolerance for being in the thick of my son's now.

When I was eleven, Jinx's age, I got hold of a contraband copy of the
sludgy novel *Peyton Place* and called up my peanut-size boyfriend and
read him salacious passages until my mother overheard and intervened. I was so mortified when she caught me that I flew into my bedroom, sobbing, and vowed to kill myself with the only weapon handy:
a hairbrush. I would swallow it whole. Then I got a better idea: poison. I would kill myself by swallowing a little vial of Cutex nail polish
remover. My mother tenderly interceded.

The twins, Gina and Dorrie Eldridge, had spin-the-bottle parties in
the rec room of their house when I was in sixth grade. I attended these
parties with gusto, hoping to get the chance to plant my lips on David
Williams's. I liked him because he was the best kickball player and
had clumpy curly hair the color of scrambled eggs. Whenever I passed
him on the bike path I'd holler, "Hi, Scrambled-Eggs-on-Top!" He

didn't mind. He even blushed. But in those days, liking a boy was lots easier than kissing one. You had to make kissing into a game to make it palatable. Boys' lips tasted and felt like earthworms, and kissing them was always more of a tomboy test than a prelude to romance.

The summer between sixth and seventh grade, Cindy Goldstein hostessed our class's first pre-meditated make-out party. We all went to it knowingly. Word had gotten out that Cindy's parents had agreed to disappear. Along with pretzels, snacks would include other people's lips. I sat nervously on a sofa beside the tallest boy in my class. By that time, everybody else was partnered, either dancing cheek-to-cheek or smooching in a corner. The lights were dim. Finally, high on pretzels, he kissed me fourteen salty seconds on the lips. Fourteen seconds. I counted them. Each was an infinity of time. And the whole while the kiss was happening, I felt myself swelling with a kind of elephantiasis of awkwardness. My hands felt clumsy and gargantuan, my chin, my nose. I couldn't figure out how or when to breathe during such a long kiss. It seemed like breathing would interrupt the momentum, would be rude, like burping. As soon as I thought about burping, I wanted to. Worst of all, I didn't know how to kiss back. All I could do was to imagine myself a pliant surface and to count slowly to fourteen, holding my breath, fighting the profoundest urge to burp, my hands at my sides, huge inflated danglings. At least I had the sense to count silently.

By the time I was thirteen, I'd taken up with a girl I will call Jenny Smithwick, whom my mother disapproved of as shifty-eyed. Jenny and I rode horses together, and Jenny's mother was a divorcee—a rarity in those days. The Smithwicks lived next door to a McDonald's. You could smell the twinkly fragrance of sizzling french fries from any room in their house. Mrs. Smithwick, energetic, blonde, with a pixie's face like her daughter's, walked around barefooted in the house. Her toenails were painted scarlet. She wore short-shorts. She smoked cigarettes and drank Champale out of cans.

Once I invited Jenny to spend the night at my house and, as if to prove my mother's suspicions were correct (that Jenny was a bad influence), she concocted a plan for us to sneak out after my parents were asleep. Everybody at school talked about their subversive late-night escapades, coups against parentally ordained curfews. But I lived in a suburban neighborhood, far from the amusements of town. There was no McDonald's close by, beckoning with its nightlife, the carnival aroma of hot french fries looping the golden arches. We could sneak out, but then what?

I remember that we scuttled from the house, wearing our long nightgowns, and that there was a full moon and we danced around in the front yard. Our nightgowns were luminous with moonlight, gauzy as cocoons: we could see the shadowy lithe pupas of our bodies moving beneath the radiant cloth. We clowned around in the street, flipped cartwheels, do-si-doed around trees in the neighbors' yards, laughing at the splendor of our wildness, falling down limp with silly derangement in the cool grass, making bug eyes, acting koo-koo, pretending we were psychopaths escaped from the insane asylum.

Such were my treacheries, my teenage transgressions: timid girl stuff. By comparison, when my teenage brothers sneaked out, they crept over to the swim club and threw all the lounge chairs in the swimming pool. Some fun! Once they climbed a service station roof and rearranged the letters TEXACO to spell A COTEX.

The crimes of youth which cast the longest shadows are the crimes of self-treason, so easy to commit because the self is in flux, hasn't solidified and won't for many years of trial and error. Because we aren't sure about who we are, it's easy to be anybody, to affect a persona that when viewed through the clarifying lens of hindsight seems more a caricature than a portrait of yearning.

One of my most memorable bouts of self-treason occurred when I was about fifteen years old, old enough by today's progressive standards to have known better. My friend Karen, a member of the Rainbow Girls service club, offered to scrounge me up a blind date with a visiting Demolay—the male counterpart organization of the Rainbows. I didn't date in high school. My popularity had peaked around sixth grade when I'd started to grow, outsizing every boy in my age group. Also, I was too earnest a young girl to be much fun on a date. Inspired by the love sonnets of Elizabeth Barrett Browning, I affected the melancholy limpness of a suffering poet.

When Karen phoned to offer me a blind date, I'm sure the chance to go out with a human boy turned me a little crazy with anticipation. Probably I bought a new party dress and laid it out days in advance. For special enhancement, my mother phoned Leon's Beauty Salon and made an appointment for me to have my hair professionally sculpted into a french twist. By 3 P.M. on the afternoon of the Rainbow Girls' dance, although my blind date hadn't yet called me to confirm our arrangement, I sat enthroned in a salon chair at Leon's while the stylist strove to concoct a new, more Audrey Hepburnish me.

It was a struggle for her. Mine was fine, limp crabgrass hair to begin with, a lackluster mustardy blonde, loaded with electricity. It was lots of trouble just to keep it smoothly combed. I hated it, and I could sense the stylist's disapproval as she lifted wispy streamers of it with her comb and began to plan her strategy.

She began teasing it, almost angry, and teased it for nearly an hour until every square inch ballooned upward and my head began to resemble a smoking soufflé. Once she began to smooth it into a helmet shape, I relaxed. The tangles were now her problem, not mine, and by her vigor I could tell that she would wrestle the mess into the shape that she'd ordained. But as I watched her struggle, I could see that she was failing. By the time she'd finished with me, the thing she'd created looked Amazonian, like, say, if King Kong had worn an Afro— except that the Afro wouldn't come into fashion for five or six more years. It looked as if some explosive device attached to my head had detonated. It rose nearly two feet off my scalp, so tall, in fact, that when my mother came to pick me up, the do wouldn't fit in the car. I had to fold myself like a pocketknife to keep it from grazing the ceiling. Mother tried not to laugh, but I could tell by her twitching expression that she thought nobody with a grain of sanity would go out in public with such a coiffeur and expect to be taken seriously. I mustered a laugh, too. I did think it was funny that I couldn't sit up straight in the car. But when I angled the rearview mirror to take a closer look, I panicked. The hairdo was so overwhelming that it looked like I had a shrunken head. Too, the stylist had sprayed about a gallon of Aqua-Net over the whole thing and it glistened like a gymnasium floor. If you want to know why there's an ozone depletion, I'd like to suggest that this hairdo was the beginning of biohazard.

It was five o'clock. My date was due to arrive at 6:30—although he still hadn't phoned to confirm. Mother promised that she had plenty of time to amend my cosmetic disaster. At least I had hair. At least I hadn't been scalped. We hurried home, where both of us worked on detangling, hacking through the briar patch of my hair with machete strokes of our combs. At one point in our hysteria I'm sure we considered butching me with Daddy's electric shaver.

Just as my mother had promised, I was ready by 6:30, my hair rearranged in a composition suggesting I was a human female. I hadn't had time to eat supper, but no matter, I would snack at the party.

By 7 my date had still not arrived. I phoned the friend who had masterminded this ordeal, but she'd already left for the dance. By 8 I was close to tears. All that trouble! All that vanity! The torment I'd undergone for a *stranger*—and all because he was a boy! Did I want some supper? No, I told my mother, no, I was going to wait it out. If I ate, I'd have to brush my teeth again and reapply lipstick. By 9 I was sobbing with disappointment, and perhaps the dim sense of having betrayed myself. If I did not begin to rip the hairpins out of my sedate french twist and stab them mercilessly into my heart, I felt like doing so—or I dreamed of it.

Compared with my own vast sagas of foolishness committed and survived, Rod's friend Jinx is probably a novice. Why is it that when I've learned so much about stupid girl stuff, I've only got sons to tell it to?

Now, inside my house, there are four teenagers, when before there was one. They have multiplied effortlessly like coat hangers in a closet. Four teenagers packed into Rod's small bedroom upstairs. I'm listen-

ing for their visit to turn rowdy. I'm sniffing the air for the furtive
odor of cigarette smoke. Maybe I'm listening, too, for remnants of
innocence: a bottle to be spun on the floor.

In the kitchen I stir the snap beans simmering in broth and ham
hocks. I sprinkle the baking chicken with a pinch more sage and put
little red-skinned new potatoes on to boil. I remove a fresh-baked loaf
of cornbread from the oven. The recipe I use makes cornbread so light
and sweet that it can double as cake. Topped with strawberries and
whipped cream, it's a dessert. Now I'm worrying about what the other
teenagers are going to eat for supper. Should I stall our supper or boot
the visitors out? The pleasant goodwill fragrances of warm, tenderhearted food make me feel generous. Should I invite the other children to eat supper with Rod and me? The notion to do so enters my
brain most sincerely. It's nearly seven o'clock. If they're all still hanging around at 7:05, I might ask.

I'm trying to discern why the girl is the problem. Girls tend to have
a subduing, civilizing effect on young teenage boys. They do so un-
knowingly, simply by wearing a sweet cologne, displaying clean
fingernails, shining hair, a dimple, unconsciously in possession of an
unassuming loftiness, the precious remoteness of a shelved figurine.
I've observed both my sons behaving with such grace and calm around
pretty young girls that I could swear they've had lobotomies or sub-
stituted trained actors proficient in impersonating upgraded, saintly
versions of themselves. I've always been too grateful for their refined
behavior to level charges of imposter at them. Maybe it's *this* girl, in
all fairness, who's the problem. She seems at loose ends with her
chipped nail polish and frayed cutoffs, floppy clogs, bare midriff, tuft
of navel winking. She wears dusky blue eye-shadow and pancake
makeup over her freckles. Where are her giggling girlfriends? *She's
only eleven years old,* the girl my mother was always warning me
against becoming. I feel the impulse to call her away from the crudery
of these boys and teach her how to make a pie crust from scratch.

If my mother knew about the spin-the-bottle parties and my
fourteen-second kiss or my brother's prankish anagram for Texaco,
she never said. She'd improvised and survived a highly mischievous
childhood herself. She would have considered departures from inno-

cence wholly normal, even necessary, as her children lurched in fits and starts toward becoming adults. I've always believed, as she must have, that in surviving our own mistakes—even the bitterest kind, of long duration—we are more resilient keepers of our own children. That is if we've been able to forgive ourselves.

Sometimes, raising teenage boys alone, I feel less kinship with my mother than with the long-horned beetle that Rod pinned for his biology project. The beetle went onto the mounting board kicking and screaming. He had only been out for a little stroll, preening his antennae, minding his own business, perhaps thinking about reading a book in the lull before dinner, when some new trouble he couldn't clearly identify snatched him up and crucified him in the name of science. What are such sacrifices to science compared with those made in the name of parenthood? Aren't we parents just out for a walk, minding our own business, opening a book, when we are suddenly pinioned by a project we hadn't fully planned or can't control and are uncertain, at best, of how our painstaking contribution will eventually be judged?

After Rod has played guitar for his visitors, they clodhop down the stairs and bang out into the big bad world in which, ultimately, they look less threatening. Outdoors they could be any old weed; inside, they're mobile poison ivy with a momentum like tumbleweed. How must they have interpreted the supper smells unraveling from my kitchen? Maybe it was the scent of nurture that ran them off. I may have seemed the sort of witch that would make them eat vegetables.

"Well," I say to Rod as he ambles downstairs, "I finally met the notorious Jinx."

"She's not so bad," he says. "She's really sort of cool—for an eleven-year-old."

"She looks plenty wild to me."

"So are the buttercups growing out in the front yard, but you don't cut them down."

He did not actually say this. I imagined that if he wanted to defend his choice in friends, he ought to have said it—and without recriminations.

"She thinks I'm pretty cool," is what he really said.

"Are you?"

"Sort of. Were you ever cool, Mom?"

"Never in my entire silly life," I say truthfully. What a relief to confess it!

"Were you a dork?"

"By today's standards. And, if truth be told, by yesteryear's as well."

"A dork," he says ruefully. I can tell he's considering the chilling possibilities of genetically mandated dorkdom.

"To be honest," I say, "back when I was in high school I didn't think about whether I was cool or not. Cool wasn't even an option. All I remember thinking about was how miserable I was that I didn't have a boyfriend."

"That's pathetic, Mom."

"I know that now."

"I'm cool," he says, "but I'm not *real* cool," he confesses, as if to keep me company on the bench. "I'd say I'm only *medium* cool. I hang out with some of the cool people at school, except I can tell the coolest guy doesn't like me. I don't know why he doesn't like me. It's weird."

"In high school it's probably a waste of time to worry about why somebody doesn't like you."

He looks a little chagrined. "I don't know why I'm telling you all this stuff," he says. "It's just junk. Cool people don't tell their parents stuff like this. Most of the people my age don't even *talk* to their parents."

"Don't worry. Dorks can't remember the stuff cool people tell them anyway."

He smiles, almost slings an arm around me in a comradely way, would have a year ago; but it's a much-needed point for cooldom that he refrains.

"What's for supper?" he says, sniffing hungrily. "I'm starving. It smells wonderful."

Wedding Music

OUR LITTLE CHICKERING grand piano reposes in the living room, at the foot of the stairs, en route to every other room in the house, and Sam, my youngest son, can't pass it without dropping onto the bench and playing a piece. All summer he's been practicing a repertoire of formal wedding music. I don't know the couple he refers to as Melanie and Scott, but they've hired him to play for their wedding in August and are going to pay him fifty dollars.

Sam's fourteen. His reedy shinbones are battered from skateboarding. Between practices at the piano he has gained a permanent dimple in his right cheek from where he flip-kicked a skateboard into his face. Besides playing piano and skateboarding, he enjoys writing poetry, composing thumpy Leonard Bersteinish rock opera tunes for the keyboard, playing basketball and Nintendo. He likes to draw, taught himself how to juggle and to walk on tall stilts. He owns a unicycle. He named his cat Edward John Dan Henry Francis and taught the cat how to box. If he finds a bug in the house, he will carry it outside to freedom rather than stomping it flat. When he was younger, he said that he could smell snakes in the woods and that they smelled

"jumbly." His most recent theory is that if you sneeze with your eyes
wide open, they'll pop out. He says it was an ancient Chinese torture.
"And where did you find this fact?" I ask. "Never mind, Mother-of-
Pearls," says Sam of the sprightly wholehearted big-hearted loud
funny life. "I just know."

I've never washed dishes to the bridal chorus from Wagner's *Lo-
hengrin,* but this summer I do. It's probably my imagination that the
dishes, freshly scrubbed and dripping in the drain, shine like a bride's
newly unpacked wedding china. Our house resonates with the plucky
bombast of Mendelssohn's "Wedding March" from *A Midsummer
Night's Dream,* and I parade up the stairs, hugging our folded laundry like a trousseau. I feel lofted by the music. It isn't about the
pinched dim domestic spaces of broom closets; it's a summons to glory,
ascendance into clear skies, the pioneering zest of Westward ho,
gleaming horizons, panoramic sunsets roaring like the furnaces of
love-fueled hearts.

When the weather is pleasant, we fling open the front door to
admit fresh air, and Sam's melodies purl outward in a voluminous
swath of fanfare. Joggers gaze in as they pass. Such rare music, drifting from an ordinary house, must sound like a visitation from an-
gels—or cherubim if you know that the notes are tumbling from a
keyboard played by a child. It's the sort of music that elicits universal
electrification of the soul. Even if you walked down the aisle to this
music and vouchsafed yourself to a doomed marriage, a few phrases of
Gounod's "Sanctus" or Purcell's "Trumpet Voluntary" recall a time
when you were not only innocent enough to believe the fairy tale but
brave enough to attempt living in it.

I was ten years old when a distant cousin, Billy Jenkins, a farmer in
Potecasi, North Carolina, married his sweetheart Audrey, and my
Grandmother Ruth wrangled me an invitation to be an attendant in
the wedding. My status was junior bridesmaid. Although I'd visited
Potecasi a few times before, I didn't know my cousins well. I remem-

bered Billy Jenkins as the colorful one: ruddy, with a sunburned nose, talkative, a trickster and a tease. Everybody else in town, other than Audrey, seemed gray and frail. Their elderly skin felt sticky when you hugged them. They hobbled slowly along with canes and scraped their corn off the cob because they wore false teeth. The men dressed in bibbed overalls and wheezed when they laughed. Some of the older women carried around discreet little cans for dipping snuff. Audrey was distinguished by her youthfulness; she wore her plain brown hair in a tight helmet of curls which suggested a recent home permanent. Billy was missing a couple of fingers due to accidents with farm equipment. More precisely, he was missing parts of digits: some of his fingers had their top thirds lopped off. I couldn't seem to train my eyes away from his stubby hands. He waved them around when he talked as if they looked perfectly normal. It seemed that he discounted the importance of having whole fingers, that he regarded whole fingers as accessories—like belts and cufflinks—rather than necessities of life.

Grandmother Ruth and I stayed at Aunt Ira and Uncle Fred's house. They were kindly, accommodating folks, but no relation whatsoever. Their two-story farmhouse was roofed in tin; the wooden floors dipped and slanted and creaked; a claw-footed bathtub hunkered in the bathroom and antimacassars festooned the living room furniture. In their back lot blustered a pugnacious bull calf they were fattening to eat. I felt sorry that it was doomed and tried to befriend it; but it brandished its budding horns at me and chased me under the barbed-wire fence.

Across the two-lane highway stood an old Shell gas station that looked like a cottage, the kind with stout brick pillars and terra cotta roof tiles. In front of the garage, teenage boys leaned into the maws of opened car hoods and disappeared into the greasy dark innards as if being eaten alive.

Beside Uncle Fred's house, in a grove of tall shade trees, was his general store. It had oiled plank floors and a stippled tin ceiling hung with black fans spidering the muggy air. On the counter sat an ornate brass cash register that looked more like a tiny throne, surrounded by tall glass jars filled with twinkling geodes of hard rock candy. A rusty little cast-iron woodstove, as sturdy and smug-looking as a goat, stood smiling in one corner of the store, leashed to a tall length of stovepipe that exited the ceiling.

Uncle Fred sold everything there: machine parts, nails, seeds, fertilizer, hoses, tools, detergent, motor oil, bolts of fabric, boots and jeans. Broad ribbons of molasses-colored flypaper trailed from the ceiling. I'd never seen flypaper before, and I was fascinated. I'd been saving my allowance to buy a Venus's-flytrap at Woolworth's back home. Uncle Fred peeled me a strip of new flypaper from a roll he kept behind the counter and told me to keep it as a souvenir.

My memory of Billy and Audrey's wedding day is a swirl of sweltering heat and pastel dresses and white straw hats afloat in the humid green air like water lilies, and the drenching fragrance of gardenia bouquets. I wore a lavender short-sleeved dress made of raspy taffeta and trimmed with dark purple velveteen ribbons. I paraded around like royalty. I even got to wear lipstick. This was, after all, my first wedding and it was about fancy clothes, steambath weather, best behavior, flypaper, a conceited little calf who had no idea that he was being fattened for slaughter, balancing a plate of food on my lap as I sat atop a floor fan in some distant relative's humid house and tried to remember to chew with my mouth shut, watermelon pickles, deviled eggs, chicken so crispily fried that it looked armored in batter, ham baked with pineapples and cherries, succotash, potato salad, cole slaw, German Johnson tomatoes soaked in vinegar and sugar, percolated coffee as black as tar, a wedding cake as tall and dribblety as a sand castle, a cool soak in a claw-footed tub with a brick of freshly opened Ivory soap, the sputter of rain falling on a tin roof, the sizzling swell of cicadas in the trees, a bridegroom without all his fingers. Even then I had the sense that a wedding wasn't about marriage at all.

The summer I was seventeen, I began to date the boy I would eventually marry. I'd never had an authentic steady boyfriend before, and although weeks lapsed between our early dates, this was the beginning of a courtship. He had two things going for him: first, he was older. Because none of my friends knew him, he seemed mysterious. Second, he drove his parents' 1952 MG-TD on our first date. We went to see *Viva Las Vegas,* starring Elvis Presley in his prime. It was summertime. I wore a yellow sleeveless seersucker dress with a straight skirt and a drawstring waist. I wore the most wonderful shoes I have every owned: a pair of sky-blue flats that laced the tops of my feet with thin crisscrossings of blue leather strings. They were Maid Marian shoes. I had worked excruciatingly hard on my hairdo, and I labored just as long picking out a protective scarf from my mother's collection to carry along in case he lowered the convertible top. It was lowered when he arrived.

After the movie, we drove to the Boar and Castle Drive-in for green drinks, specialty nonalcoholic limeades. My date referred to the Boar and Castle as "the adolescent hangout." He spoke with the superior calculated derision of James Bond. He was nineteen. He peered down his nose when he made his pronouncements. It was a long, narrow, aquiline nose, highly suited for a pince-nez. It was a nose that sat in judgment, its hauteur fixed by nostrils flared like wing nuts. I'm afraid that, at seventeen, I regarded the nose and the stance that it took as majestic. I did not possess an aloof bone in my body, and going out with a boy who did felt brazen and cynical. I was too sweet. Everybody I knew was too sweet. Unapologetically jeerful, this boy was antidotal to sweet. That he so bluntly expressed his disdain for people and places he considered beneath him gave him an aura of sophistication. I was a sucker for aura.

The last wedding I served in as a bridesmaid (before I starred in my own) was another distant cousin's (also a relative of Grandmother Ruth's). I'd gotten to know Rachel, an attractive schoolteacher, when she'd roomed at my grandmother's while finishing her practice-teaching assignment in Greensboro. She was engaged to marry a

handsome naval officer named Hal—she had a picture of him in his
uniform. Whenever Rachel talked to me about Hal, I filled with foggy
yearning. How was this possible when I already had a boyfriend?

I was eighteen and would attend college in the fall. My boyfriend
and I had been discussing whether or not we should date other people,
since we would be living in different towns and neither of us owned
cars. I was suspicious that such discussions implied we were sneakily
dissatisfied with our current arrangement and were weakly trying to
separate. Why would we want to date other people except to make
comparisons? I'm sure I must have put the question to his face, in a
grievous burst of piety. But if you felt that you needed to make comparisons, the implication was that you lacked confidence in your selection, right?

I drove my grandmother down to Littleton for the wedding preliminaries. I felt restless and glum. I wanted something to happen. At
home I'd begun to pick arguments with my mother. We fought over
the mess I made of the bathroom we shared, and I passionately defended my right to make messes. The August air felt turgid and filmy.
If there were shooting stars, they eked across the sky and left the
slowly luminous mucilage of snails. Wavelets of heat rose from the
streets, or originated inside hearts—it was impossible to tell the source.
My boyfriend, writing me a letter from summer school, had asked if
he could call me Marian because he preferred that name to my own.

In Littleton, I met Rachel's younger brother, whom everybody
called by his nickname, "Bro" (pronounced "Brrrruh" in a drawling
way). He was a couple of years older than I, a fraternity boy enrolled
at the University in Chapel Hill. Like his sister he was tall, dark-
haired, abundantly freckled, smiley, and courteous. Rachel clearly
adored him. I remember the pair of them mugging for a picture, their
arms draped around each other's shoulders with companionable languor. They looked lucky.

We played croquet while other guests, seated on lawn furniture,
sipped cocktails. Across the sloping twilit yard, fireflies swung their
tiny lanterns. The whites of blouses and shirts and teeth and socks
glowed with ethereal brilliance and seemed, after a while, to float as if

disembodied upon the darkening air. Little bats swooped and darted
overhead. Torches were lit. The aroma of meat sizzling on the grill
mingled with the rhapsodic lovesick fragrance of roses on a trellis. I
felt myself sliding deeper into wonderment.

I relaxed around Bro. My defenses melted until I felt happily
sloppy, not guarded or calculating. He made me laugh, snortingly, and
I didn't bother to subdue such a laugh with a hand clamped over my
mouth. That I didn't feel scrutinized, sentence by sentence (the way
my boyfriend measured me in social situations), put me at ease. I was
not trying to impress Bro, and I marveled that just my plain true self
wielded charm in this lovely fresh country. I understood that Bro had
a girlfriend, that she was arriving the next day to stay for the remain-
der of the wedding festivities. I regretted that she was coming but felt
uncertain why. Sometimes I would catch Bro's eye and imagine that he
regretted it, too.

"I've really had a great time," he said at the end of the evening.
"Sally's coming tomorrow, but we can still have fun." Did he mean to
suggest that he resented his chains? Maybe he was soliciting a show
of honesty on my part, encouraging me to admit that I resented my
chains as well. But I didn't have the sense to know that I resented
them. I was simply enjoying the lavish attention of his company, the
conspiracy to have fun with a boy who did not appear to want anything else from me. Certainly he had no plan to drag me out and away
from my true self for reform or redefinition. I imagined that his kiss
would be unencumbered by the feints and strategies of seduction—a
pal kiss, not a greedy one—and, briefly, I wished that Bro was my
boyfriend. In that instant of wishing he was and betraying my
boyfriend because of the wish, I should have known what was in store
for me. I should have known that I wasn't ready to become formally
engaged at the tender age of eighteen, that I was in love with hope
and possibilities—not any boy—and in a moony, moralistic, sticky
way. I was as vulnerably nondiscriminating as a strip of flypaper, dangling myself out in the breeze.

At school, in my English classes, I'd loaded up my heart with
the thematic admonitions of *The Scarlet Letter, Romeo and Juliet,*

Kate Chopin's *The Awakening,* "The Love Song of J. Alfred Pru-frock," and I believed that love was *supposed* to make you forlorn. Love was necessarily tinged with tragedy, lest you had heaven on earth. It was about martyrdom, missed connections, good intentions misconstrued, deceit, betrayal, devastating jealousy, denial, punish-ment, horrendous torture and sacrifice, the iron press of fate—even death. As antidote, I'd gorged on fatally high doses of Elizabeth Bar-rett Browning—not merely her love poems, but all the letters she'd written to Robert, an intemperate palaver of gush and yearning, penned while she lay in bed, an invalid. There for awhile I took up the habit of writing my boyfriend letters by candlelight, in lagoon-green ink, and sealing the envelopes with dollops of sealing wax so red and fatly puckered that it looked as if I were mailing him my lips.

Part of staying true to my boyfriend was to prove to my family and friends that I hadn't made a mistake, that I'd walked methodically to the edge of reason, positioned myself with authority, and swan-dived into what I perceived as a clear, calm pool. If the pool I'd aimed for turned out to be quicksand, hadn't I learned in Girl Scouts how to rescue myself? Don't agitate. Relax. Roll over on your back. Flatten yourself.

I was confident that I was acting on my own, but I was not. I was acting according to the mandates of a phantom self, an imagined me with the accommodating margins of a cloud. My enthusiasm for spreading myself too thin was boundless. Steeped in the bravado of nurture—a birthright made possible by kindly parents who had given me no trouble—I had happiness to burn. I felt spendthrift with it. If my boyfriend had not been so possessive, I could have married the whole world. To marry the world is precisely what a young girl feels capable of at the height of her powers. The boy who leads such a girl prematurely down the aisle is probably headed for drastic disap-pointment.

We forget all this at the weddings of the young. Perhaps the per-sistence of hope is every wedding's gift to every guest. *Here comes the bride.* In spite of any doubts she may have suffered, despite a recent misunderstanding with the groom over, say, who has the longest, most judgmental nose (a disagreement that she suspects might be the genesis of the final argument that will wreck them), she floats down the aisle with the dazed serenity of an amnesiac, flaunting determination: trailblazer in lace.

❧

The wedding for which Sam will provide music is the second wedding he's performed in. The first was his father's, several years ago. His father married a psychologist who, as a method of healing and unification, requested involvement of all the disparate stepchildren in the marriage ceremony. This was the psychologist's third marriage. Her most recent husband had died about a year earlier, and his children (her stepchildren) were struggling to comprehend how their stepmother could replace their beloved father so quickly. My own much younger children had expressed only elation that their father seemed tranquil again.

The psychologist, also an amateur actress, delights in spectacle, family pageants with herself in the starring role. Her wedding festivities were extravagant enough to divert even the most skeptical stepchild from the discomforts of forced new alliances. Friends who attended told me that everybody had a wonderful time, that all the children, downy with candlelight, looked lovely and brave, and that after the ceremony—for which Sam both ushered and played the piano—guests at the reception danced themselves silly and feasted on a catered gourmet supper. Such an abundance of fun was had that nobody noticed when the party was over and the marriage began.

There's no reason for Sam to feel the onus of what a marriage celebrates and signifies: the public boast that a particular union will endure. It wouldn't occur to him to ponder the obvious everyday ironies: that sacred vows exchanged are not, through the years, immutable; that love between men and women is rarely as unconditional as the love men and women bestow upon their children; that it's easiest and most treacherous to love when one is young and uninformed; that lovers taking one another for granted, however wearisome, is one definition of long-term love. Standing at the altar on their wedding day, a couple shares as pristine an equilibrium as they may ever know.

We watch the bride moving down the aisle as closely as we would watch a dove bloom out of thin air and alight on a magician's fingertips. Here she comes, attached as lightly to her father's sleeve. Her quiet lacy advance suggests a perishable snowy grace. She's the dove in reverse: a vanishing act in slow-motion. Gently her father separates her from his arm and guides her towards the groom. The groom pivots to claim her at the instance she materializes, undetectably, into a wife.

Sam and I pass through the church kitchen en route to the sanctuary where the rehearsal is under way. A thin young matron in a pastel dress is setting up for the rehearsal dinner. She shakes out red paper cloths over two banquet-length folding tables and sets nosegays of bright plastic flowers as centerpieces for each table. A toddler in a frilly pinafore and patent leather shoes runs up and down the length of the kitchen, amused by the clobbering sound of her little feet on the beige tile floor. She's pretending that she's a freshly shod horse. It's summertime and probably a rare event for her feet to be encased in hard shoes. She looks over her shoulder as she darts up and down, imagining a wake of dust kicked up by her stampede.

In the sanctuary, the bride-to-be, wearing a ponytail and shorts, jogs up and down the aisle, instructing her attendants about the correct cadence of the two-step promenade, matching girls with their escorts, advising them where they should stand and when to unburden her of her bouquet or adjust the train of her wedding dress. "It's a very long train," she says happily, as if she's a bird of rare plumage bragging about her tail. "Oh *good!* Sam's here," she says. I glance around the church, trying to spot the groom, but every boy in the room looks underage. She links arms with one of them and prances down the aisle, but her escort turns out to be her father.

It's a long and jolly practice, like grown-ups playing make believe without costumes. The bride begs to rehearse again and again, and her exuberance seems contagious. Nobody claims to be hungry, although it's nearly eight o'clock. All of the bridesmaids are having a dreamy time, too, imagining when their own weddings will be and who they will marry out of all the wide world. I sniff the rehearsal dinner being patiently reheated: it smells like pizza.

It's almost dark before Sam and I start for home. We're worn out and famished ourselves. Back home, for the first night since his wedding music practices began, Sam avoids the piano. Upstairs he makes origami objects out of special printed papers. He says they're housewarming gifts for his godmother, who is newly separated from her husband of twenty-five years and moving into our neighborhood. He folds tulips out of glistening foil, sailboats, a conch shell, baskets, an uncaged bird, unburstable bubbles, a modernistic table and four matching chairs that remind me, stylistically, of Frank Lloyd Wright. Think about it: nothing you'd pack to take on your honeymoon, but many useful items to help you to achieve a satisfying, redecorated and freshly directed life. The ornate ivory bride does not turn out, and so, undaunted, he constructs a crisp nun in black and white.

❧

Of course I'm invited to this wedding of strangers. I'm the musician's mother and Chief-of-Transportation. I dress up like a bona fide wedding guest. Sam attires himself in khaki slacks, a navy blazer, blue shirt, red paisley tie, and his nearly new Airwalks, hip dude skater shoes. He's left his leather church shoes at his dad's.

"They might come hear me play," he tells me on the drive to the church. "Dad and Jean."

"Okay by me."

"They might or they might not."

"Guess you'll just have to wait and see."

"But you're going to stay, aren't you?"

"I'm there for the duration, pal."

"Can we go to the reception? Melanie said I was invited. There's going to be wedding cake and tons of good food."

"Okay, we'll go for a little while."

He takes a deep breath and wipes his hands, sweaty with nerves, on his trousers. "I hope I see Dad. I mean, if he comes."

"They'll be easy to spot in a crowd," I say. "Jean will be wearing some UFO of a hat."

He doesn't laugh. He knows that I think Jean's an insufferable show-off, but he strives to think the best of everyone, even to his own detriment. I detect that the thought of all us Montagues and Capulets crashing somebody else's wedding day makes him a bit uneasy. His expression turns meditative, grave. His heartbeat seems to me as audible as a miner's pick dislodging lodestones of potential trouble.

"Everything's going to be fine," I tell him, patting his hand "I promise I won't embarrass you."

"I'll embarrass you if I don't play well."

"Nervous?"

"A little."

"A little nervous is good. It keeps you alert."

Using the rearview mirror, he straightens his tie. His shirt is too small, so snug across his chest that I can see the pickets of his ribcage. His wrist bones protrude the size of acorns. He's thin, knobby, lanky, and small, much too small for the voluminous music he makes. How does he emerge from its seizure unharmed?

In the foyer of the church wafts the chilly perfume of flowers; the air has the cool, guarded smell of a vault. A groomsman pins a burgundy cloth rose to Sam's lapel. The groomsmen, in black tuxedos, wear burgundy cummerbunds. The bridesmaids' dresses are slim sleeveless burgundy sheaths that match their rose bouquets. Having arrived early, we dawdle outside the sanctuary, chat with the bride's parents, who seem much younger than I. The bride's mother tells me that she married at seventeen, but her daughter, Melanie, has waited until nineteen. "A big improvement," she says.

Sam has instructions to begin playing a series of Bach inventions at 2:30 while guests arrive and are seated. He takes several deep breaths, swipes his hands dry on his khakis. His mahogany-colored hair gleams, so solemnly slicked down and parted that I feel a little sob in my throat as he departs for his lonesome artist's voyage to the front of the church, where the piano is prominently displayed. His showboat hands dangle at his sides; his bigfoot Airwalks bear him away. Watching his ratchety amble, nobody could guess the virtuosity, perched like a polished jewel, inside the little velvet box of his heart.

When he begins to play, the congregation materializes as if on cue: stout middle-age women escorted by shriveled-up men, babies hauled into church in their car seats along with gaudy diaper bags, saucy younger women with tall teased hair, old men with cigarette faces, melted-looking by life. There's a cowboy with a ponytail, wearing boots and jeans. The groom's mother glides down the aisle on the arm of an usher; she's wearing a black dress. I've never seen a member of the wedding family dressed in black. Is her dress a form of protest? By comparison, the bride's mother looks pert as a bird in her burgundy dress that matches the bridesmaids'. "I'm not going to cry at Melanie's wedding," she told me in the foyer. "When my oldest daughter got married, I cried and cried. But this one, well, we're just so thankful that she's his problem now. Whew!" she said, "that little gal was a wild one."

Sam's music darts and trills, even the most somber chords leaking light until the air of the church is spangled with sound and the amber preserve of candlelight, prismatic dapplings of sun sieved through stained-glass windows. The immortal strivings of Bach arc over all as if to construct a transparent cathedral unbound by walls or ceilings: music as purest church, supple centuries-old conduit to God.

I watch as Sam maneuvers his way through the labyrinthine fugues with wit and awe and something like mischievousness when he plays an extended trill or darts a tricky finger to high C as if he's snatching up a wayward pickup stick. It's all there in the music: the humble and the lofty, sprites and God, the holy and the cow, exultations of miracles and the whole sob story of humanity.

The congregation shushes its loud crackle of florid dresses, the shuffle of shoes, the booming whispers of small children, the wag of handshakes and hugs as the bridesmaids lilt down the aisle. Once they've assembled at the front of the church, Sam pauses, bows his head. The silence is so profound that you can hear dust motes twirling down the golden air and chiming wherever they settle. A door in the chancel opens and the minister, accompanied by the groom—a thin, balding boy, stoop-shouldered, tucking himself, turtle-esque, as far inside his tux as its stricture will allow—enter and take positions and gaze as if into dreamy vistas down the aisle as Sam begins the "Bridal Chorus" announcing Melanie's stately promenade.

And when Melanie appears—I don't even know her last name—I believe that she's the most beautiful bride I've ever seen. Watching her face is like probing the plush inner spiral of a rosebud about to open. Her waist is as tiny as a child's.

I hear the undulations of her gown, frothing like foam on a lapping wave. Her stride is confident, proud, her posture erect on this maiden voyage, bold and serene as a ship's figurehead. She holds her father's sleeve lightly, ready to give him up. One reason we cry at weddings is, of course, because of the music: its intricate entwinement of proclamation and prayer, the gallant and the frail, majesty and innocence, flight without a net. It is the swiftness of the music breaking over us, like the bride dancing past, that disarms and reminds us that life is a constant collusion between our rush toward glory and our cadenced regrets.

In less than fifteen minutes, the service is over and Mr. and Mrs. scamper up the aisle, relief on their faces. Sam plays the plucky Mendelssohn while the congregation files out. That's when I turn and glimpse sight of them: Sam's father and his second wife standing at the back of the church, their gaze as distant and enigmatic as totems. The psychologist dons her couture sombrero and her husband, throttled by a colorful bowtie, sports a plantation-style suit that looks rumpled with leisure.

The three of us are clones of the uninvited thirteenth fairy who crashed the party given for Beauty in the fairy tale and laid upon the baby a curse. We represent the dregs of marital unity: leftovers, hand-me-downs, cringing where there was once embrace. No wonder Sam worried about our attendance, our warty imperfections an embarrassment to him on this most happy occasion, our being there a reminder of patchy new families, failed love, proof that shiny new lovers can turn into toads.

I disappear discreetly into an alcove and let the two of them privately congratulate Sam. By the time I return to the foyer, they've disappeared without so much as a puff of smoke and everybody's unscathed. "Let's eat!" Sam says gaily, striding past me on his way to the reception. We load our plates with pale moon-shaped cookies and florets of broccoli and cauliflower and a concoction called Kahlua Cake (Cool Whip, nuts, chocolate bits, pineapple chunks, Maraschino cherries, and Kahlua—the bride's sister gave me the recipe). Sam and I are both awash in punch made with raspberry sherbet with Sprite poured over it. While Sam eats, refills his plate, eats some more, I make small talk with the minister. I also chat with the bride's mother who, just as she'd predicted, didn't shed a single tear.

"Now what happens to them?" Sam asks after a lull on our drive home.

"They live happily ever after, of course."

"Do you know something, Mother-of-Pearls? I think they will."

"So do I."

"You do not. Tell the truth."

"I think that in this particular case, your music cast a spell over them."

"Really?"

"Yes really."

"I like this day," he says, loosening his tie. He switches on the radio and scrolls stations. I hear the sputtering snatch of an oldie goldie: *Believe in the magic of a young girl's soul,* wails the chorus amid a quaver of tambourines. Sam locates an alternative rock station as antidote. A group called Matchbox 20 is singing: *I want to push you around, well I will, yes I will, I want to push you down, I want to take you for granted.*

I'm thinking that maybe it was the love songs of my generation that suckered and fueled our naive little combustible hearts. Maybe the

growly knockabout songs my children's hearts steep in are better reality checks.

"Mom, do you think you'll ever get married again?"

"I don't know. Maybe. When the time is right. Who knows?"

"Can I play the piano in your wedding if you do?"

"On one condition."

"Okay."

"That you cast a spell over us, too."

He grins, presses back in his seat, his expression balmy. Sunlight
falling on his face bronzes him like a keepsake.

"Mom?" he says. "You were right."

"About what?"

"Her hat."

"Oh."

"It was humongous. It made me think of Taco Bell."

"Si, señor, but it made her easy to spot."

"True."

All the windows are rolled down as we drive home, the hot buoy-
ant air of late summer thawing the churchiness out of our bones. "I'm
going to learn more wedding music," he says. "It's fun playing at weddings. It's easy money because I like the job." He laughs the sort of
gleeful, anticipatory laugh of somebody high on a glimpse of bright
prospects. How wondrous that I am the mother of somebody this
good, somebody inquisitive, sunny, hopeful, and true. Is there any
greater consolation or forgiveness for being who I once was in all my
mistaken identity? Is there any greater prize for being human?